EXPLORING PACIFIC COAST TIDEPOOLS

by
Vinson Brown
and
Ane Rovetta

Come hear the chuckle and the laugh
where ripples foam within the pool;
Come hear the roar and thunderous boom
on reefs where creaming combers rule;
All from the same vast breathing drawn,
rhythm and heart-pulsing of the sea,
The glorious song of wave and tide
from Carmel world-circling to Dundee.

Naturegraph Publishers

Library of Congress Cataloging-In-Publication Data
Brown, Vinson, 1912–1991
   Exploring Pacific Coast Tidepools / by Vinson Brown and Ane
Rovetta. – Rev. and expanded ed.
   p.   cm.
   Includes bibliographical references and indexes.
   ISBN 0-87961-217-7 (alk. paper)
   1. Tide pool animals–Pacific Coast (U.S.) Identification.
2. Tide pool plants–Pacific Coast (U.S.)–Identification.   3. Tide
pool ecology–Pacific Coast (U.S.)   I. Rovetta, Ane. II. Title.
QH104.5.P32B76   1996
574.979–dc20   96-6085
                                                    CIP

ISBN 0-87961-217-7

Revised and Expanded Edition
Text by Vinson Brown.
Black and white illustrations by Ane Rovetta.
Color photography in "Down Where the Waves Talk,"
   Ernest Braun.
Photographers for "Systematic List of Plants and Animals" are
   listed on page v.

Books for a better world

Naturegraph Publishers, Inc.
3543 Indian Creek Road
Happy Camp, CA 96039 U.S.A.

Table of Contents

PART I

PART II

List of Color Plates

-1- Girl and bat star (276), *Patiria miniata*, at Point Bolinas

Adventures and Thrills on Rocky Shores

In the blazing sunlight, in the mist of morning, in the coolness of night, the rocky shores and tidepools of our Pacific coast offer a glimpse into the strange and beautiful wilderness of the underwater world. Only along this narrow ribbon where land, sea, and air meet can we easily enter the kingdom of the sea, using our feet, hands, ears and eyes to explore and discover. With the sharp tang of sea air in our lungs, and the boom of waves or the sigh of foam on rockweed in our ears, we venture bravely into the unknown. Our adventures and discoveries will be limited only by our curiosity and the incoming tide.

Let us sit down by the edge of the rocky shore and be still for awhile, watching and listening. As we try to catch the mood of the sea and its life, we become aware that the surface appearances around us are far from a true picture of what is there. Mother Sea is a food basket to the creatures of the shore, a great giver of sea milk to her children. Twice a day the wavelets sigh higher on the beaches, talking and chuckling in and out of the tidepools, teasing the long flowing tresses of the seaweed, and rising and falling in the pools. This is the tide coming in with plankton, tiny animals and plants invisible to us except through a microscope, but as vital to the shore animals as a rich soup would be to a starving man. Mussels, clams, barnacles, and other creatures wait for the coming of this life-giving plankton, which they capture with tubes, mouths, or the fine filaments of gills or tentacles.

We cannot see this feeding, but we can imagine it: we can sit back and begin to visualize the complexity of the web of life along the shore in front of us. There are not only the many plankton-feeders, but also those which feed on seaweed and algae; the hunters, such as the shellfish and the starfish; the scavengers, such as the crabs and sea roaches; and the parasites, such as the worms who live in and on the bodies of other creatures. During the daytime, especially, much of this life is hidden in crevices, under seaweed, and under rocks. The tidepool into which we peer may appear at first almost lifeless except for the seaweed and a few obvious creatures like sea anemones and seastars. If we sit and watch for awhile, we may begin to see little fish which dart about between clumps of seaweed, their upper bodies so darkly camouflaged as to appear part of the weeds; an almost transparent shrimp which flashes across an open space in the water, or a delicate lacy nudibranch which walks upside down just under the surface, clinging through surface tension. If we continue to watch closely, we may see that those things we thought were just dark bumps on the rock are actually limpets or turban snails; one of the latter may suddenly become lively in a very unsnaillike way because the shell is occupied by a hermit crab, one of the clowns of the seashore. If we are brave enough to wade into the water of the pool and turn over rocks (always putting each one back into place after studying the life under it), or lift up the seaweed to look inside or beneath it, being careful of the powerful pincers of the kelp crab, we may find even more curious creatures, such as peanut worms, ghost crabs, sea spiders, or skeleton shrimps, children of many hidden worlds of life.

The adventure lies not only in finding new life, but in seeing life in intimate detail. For example, by fixing up a bucket or waterproof box with a glass bottom, or even swimming in the tidepools with a snorkel and face mask, we will be introduced to life obscured by the surface fluctuation of wave and foam; the glass brings us into a quiet world where the clear water shows in detail the feelers and other items of anatomy of strange creatures who move like actors on a stage. Often ignorant of being watched, they enact all the dramas of life and death. Soon we become aware that all life along the shore revolves around four vital experiences: finding food, escaping from enemies, avoiding being dried up, and reproducing. Each animal reacts differently, yet somewhat similarly, to these four experiences, and each is adapted to a particular niche in the tidepool habitat. To see these creatures and understand their activities is to be like a god who watches over the children of his creation and partakes with joy and sorrow in their triumphs and defeats. Adventures and thrills indeed can fill our every minute!

To Save and Protect

We cannot enter this wilderness paradise without a warning: It cannot *remain* a paradise unless we who wander on the shore remember that to see, listen, and touch is far better than to lift up and destroy. If we watch carefully along the beaches to compare the places of life with the places of death, we can understand. The web of life along our rocky shores hangs in delicate balance, easily upset by our clumsy or wanton foolishness. Whole beaches of our Pacific shores lie stripped of life, barren, and ugly, because someone dumped oil or other waste nearby or turned over rocks to see the life beneath, but never thought to turn the rocks back.

Priceless beauty may continue to be lost unless we dedicate ourselves in increasing numbers to preserving the life of our beaches. The creatures of the shores feel, even as we do, and are part of the great circle of life to which we all belong. When we turn over a rock, the animals underneath are exposed to an environment of heat and light for which they are not adapted, and soon will die, unless we remember to return the rock to its original position. So preserve and conserve the delightful life of our shores. Take photographs instead of specimens, and teach others also not to destroy, for great treasures cannot last where destroyers come.

It is ignorance more than evil that causes people to destroy or hurt beautiful things. A false economy may work its harmful effects when sewage or oil is dumped where it destroys the life of beaches, or when the waste products of industry, especially chemical firms, are allowed to contaminate stretches of the shore. We, as individuals, may feel helpless to stem this kind of insidious destruction, but the history of our nation has shown that time and again an aroused public opinion can force politicians and government officials to initiate policies that change conditions that had become wrong or intolerable. When we discover circumstances along the shore that are leading to the destruction of life we can not only write to our representatives in government about this, but join with such conservation-spreading organizations as the Sierra Club and the National Audubon Society, which fight to save wildlife and beauty.

There is a story about two ladies who both had beautiful flower gardens. One was constantly badgered by neighborhood children throwing rocks in her garden or otherwise harming it. The second lady, however, never had any such trouble, because, instead of warring with the children and threatening them as did the first, she took them into her garden and taught them to appreciate the beauty of the individual flowers. If we find people destroying life on the beach, we should direct them away from this evil by wisely and tactfully showing them how much more interesting the life on the shore is alive than dead.

How to Use This Book

The new edition of this book is meant to be a field guide to more complete identification, to help you recognize most of your findings, and to point the way to many more. Although focusing mainly on tidepool life, this book also covers much of the life in eelgrass flats and in open rocks.

Through continuing use of the text to identify different species of seashore life you will gradually increase your knowledge and your ability to identify what you see. Sometimes different species are so much alike that it is difficult to differentiate between them, so in the descriptions we try to give special characteristics to look for that will help to distinguish the differences. The line drawings are placed as closely as possible to the species descriptions; the color plates are attached by name and number to the part of the book where their descriptions can be found. Sometimes just the habitats where the animals and plants live will help you to differentiate among two or three species of the same genus that look very much alike. For example, the noisy pistol shrimp (*Alpheus clamator*) looks almost exactly like the California pistol shrimp (*Alpheus californiensis*), but *clamator* is found among the coastal rocks, while *californiensis* is found on mud flats in bays and estuaries. In cases where you cannot identify a species, make a guess and then later try to ask an expert. Keep trying, and gradually you will become an expert yourself.

Zones, Habitats, and Niches of Life

The rocky shores have zones, niches, and habitats where life varies greatly in its adaptations; this is shown in the outline below, and in the illustration on page 13. Keep this arrangement of life in mind as you explore the glory of the shore.

I. Outer Rocks (where the sea bursts on rocks in full fury).
  A. Tidal Zones
   1. High tide zone and splash zone (where the animals must constantly fight against the danger of drying up, and usually are protected by tough armor).
   2. Middle tide zone.
   3. Low tide zone.
  B. Niches of Various Organisms in Each Zone
   1. On the surface of rocks and not covered by seaweed.
   2. Hidden in mussel beds.
   3. Hidden under or in seaweed.
   4. Hidden in the crevices of rocks.
   5. Hidden in substratum under rocks.
   6. Free swimming in tidepools.

II. Inner Rocks (where animals are protected from the full force of the waves, usually by rocky islands, headlands, etc.).
  A. Tidal Zones
   1. High tide zone and splash zone.
   2. Middle tide zone.
   3. Low tide zone.
  B. Niches same as above.

When animals and plants are described, they will be identified with one of these zones, habitats, or niches, so that you will know where to look for them. The habitats and niches of the intertidal zone, such as the substratum (mud and sand) under a rock, are simply the places where different animals are best adapted for living. For example, the flat, long body and numerous pseudopodia (short false legs) of the mussel worm (*Nereis vexillosa*) perfectly adapt it for crawling through the crevices between mussels in a mussel bed and also for hanging on tightly when a great wave smashes against the rock. The ochre, or common, seastar (*Pisaster ochraceus*) has such a tough, leathery body and such powerful, sucking-tube feet that it does not need protection from the sea or from other animals. It can cling to exposed rock faces, withstanding all but the greatest fury of the sea.

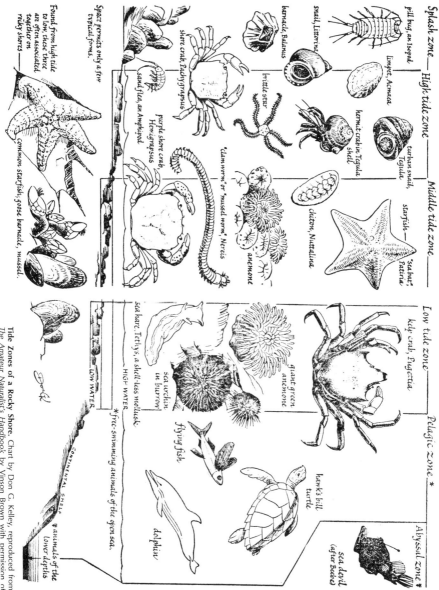

Tide Zones of a Rocky Shore. Chart by Don G. Kelley, reproduced from *The Amateur Naturalist's Handbook* by Vinson Brown with permission of the publishers, Little, Brown and Co.

-2- Exploring at ebb tide at Point Bolinas
-3- Boy reflected in tidepool
-4- Feather boa kelp (11), *Egregia menziesii*

Down Where the Waves Talk

Each living creature and plant on the shore is a distinct individual worthy of much curious watching and study. The bat star (*Patiria miniata*) (plate 1) gets it name from its webbed rays, and is uniquely adapted to living in crevices and caves among protected rocks, or under or on the many kinds of rockweed from the middle tide zone down to the low tide zone. If you put one of these on top of some wet seaweed in the shade for one to four hours during its usual breeding season from May to July, it may discharge a profusion of ripe sperm or eggs. The eggs, fertilized by the fresh sperm from a male bat star, can be kept overnight in clean glass dishes, where they will develop into tiny larvae which swim about by waving their hairlike cilia. It is a delightful experience to watch these larvae turn gradually into young seastars.

Plate 2, of young explorers searching low tidepools at ebb tide on the shore at Bolinas in Marin County, portrays innocent wonder, adventure and learning. Such a picture could also be a portent of tragedy, for if they extend their explorations to the outer rocks on a day when the great waves are piling in at the head of the long Pacific swells, the danger exists that a large wave could sweep an unlucky and unwatchful human being out to death in the sea. Wise explorers of the beaches leave the outer rocks alone when the waves are big; even when the waves are medium-sized, they are cautious enough to have companions along with them and to put a rope around the one who looks into the outermost pools.

The boy reflected in the tidepool (plate 3) is holding a hermit crab (*Pagurus*), one of those funny little clowns that occupy the shells of creatures like the black turban snail; they duck deep into their shells when you hold them in your hand, until their insatiable curiosity forces them to cautiously poke their heads out. Beyond his reflection wavering on the water is a world of Lilliputian life where shrimp and crab, rockpool Johnny and seastar, mussel, limpet, and sea urchin play their dramatic parts in a mixture of comedy and tragedy as vast as life itself and as tiny as the pool into which he is peering.

The seaweeds and rockweeds of the shore form a glorious jungle, whose mazes you could puzzle over and explore for a lifetime without coming to the end of new discoveries. So many and varied are these kinds of marine plant life that one book alone, *Marine Algae of the Monterey Peninsula*, by Gilbert M. Smith, has 688 pages devoted to that small area! Besides these very simple and primitive plants there are the surf and eel grasses, which are more evolved and complex plants that have adapted themselves to life on the edge of the sea. All such plants provide protection, hiding places, and hunting grounds for swarms of small life, even more extensive in number and kind, whose lives are often as little-known by scientists as the life there may be on other planets.

In plate 4, the detail of the surface of one of the common rockweeds of our shore is shown. The brown feather boa kelp (*Egregia menziesii*) has chocolate brown stems covered with small greenish brown tubercles, or "leaves." Actually, as with all seaweeds, these are not true stems or leaves, because the cell structure of the two parts is not different. The same simple algae cells are found in both. This plant, exceedingly common in low tidepools, often forms dense masses inhabited by many varieties of life.

One seaweed, often seen in the splash pools at the very limit or above the high tide zone, might make one imagine the shining, yellow-green hair of stranded mermaids. This has no common name, so I will call it yellow-green hairweed (*Enteromorpha intestinalis*) (plate 5). It is a wonder how it adapted itself to living in the warm and brackish water (salt mixed with fresh) of these higher pools. If you look closely, you may see tiny red dots swimming among the long strings of the seaweed. When looked at with a magnifying glass, these appear as fat, round creatures, with four pairs of hairy swimming legs. They are the splashpool copepods, *Tigriopus californicus*.

One of the delights of exploring along the rocky shores is entering secret rooms behind the rocks where the waves of centuries have worn chambers, which now echo with the endless whisper, gurgle, and mutter of the sea. Sometimes

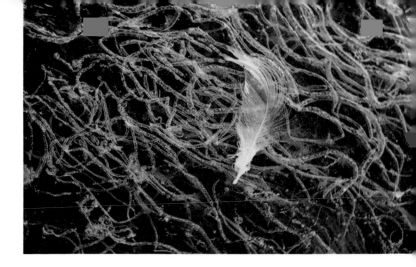

-5- Yellow-green hairweed (1),
    Enteromorpha, and white feather

-6- Two seaweeds: grapestone (26),
    Gigartina, and sea sac (28),
    Halosaccion

-7- Sunlight shining through surfgrass
    (32), *Phyllospadix*

-8- Tide ebb with iridescent seaweed (27), *Iridaea cordata splendens*

-9- Down to the caves by the sea

these are old caves whose ceilings fell in long ago, but where life, protected by the rocks from the full force of the waves, gathers in profusion. In plate 6, a lone explorer enters such a place, perhaps to gaze at the shinglelike leaves of grapestone (*Gigartina*), which cover the rocks and hide beneath their surfaces a zoo of living things.

The surfgrass (*Phyllospadix*) (plate 7) is not a seaweed, as many think, but a genuine grass that lives on the edge of the sea. It is found on the rocky shores, where inlets of other well-protected places produce the kind of sandy mud substratum it needs, and where the similar eelgrass (*Zostera*) can grow. Together they produce a unique grass habitat for several specialized animals: various kinds of hydroids (looking often like little transparent cups with flowerlike tentacles); very tiny nudibranches, or sea slugs, which feed on the hydroids; the fixed jellyfish (*Haliclystus*); various kinds of small snails, including the white bubble snail (*Haminoea*); tiny limpets; transparent and grass shrimps; the jackknife clam (*Solen sicarius*); and innumerable worms which writhe in among the roots.

Taken underwater, the picture illustrates the fantastic beauty of the surfgrass with its delicate stems waving amidst shafts of light, a veritable jungle, through which move the hunters and the hunted.

Few more glorious sights can be seen along the shore than that of the iridescent seaweed (*Iridaea cordata splendens*) (plate 8), its long, flat, leaflike fronds undulating in the ebbing waters of a large tidepool. The iridescent purple colors often pulsate and shimmer like the Northern Lights. One of the joys of surf-watching is to sit on a rock near a pool or channel, watching the play of light and color as the waves cream in and out with the long, shuddering crash and sigh of the sea.

Each seaweed has an individuality, from the green sea lettuce (*Ulva*) to all the varieties of brown, red, green, and purple rockweeds. Seaweeds can be taken home and dried in boxes between layers of sand, and then mounted with glue on flat sheets and framed under glass to decorate your home, bringing it the strange, wild feel of the sea.

When the tide ebbs, leaving the brown rocks glistening with water drops, and the crabs retreat into their crevices, go down to the caves and explore their dim interiors, taking a flashlight (plate 9). Perhaps you will find the gorgeous red sponge (*Ophlitaspongia pennata*), with its velvety surface and star-shaped openings, or some of the bright purple or other gaily colored tunicates, which look like clusters of club-headed toadstools. Often found feeding on the red sponges is the tiny, half-inch-long, bright red nudibranch (*Rostanga pulchra*), a shell-less snail, its beautiful camouflage making it look like part of the sponge. You will find many other treasures if you look in the crevices and under the rocks (always turning the rocks back to give shelter to their living jewels).

Most rocks, especially in the high tide zone, are covered with the common, dingy gray acorn barnacle (*Balanus glandula*), which looks like a tiny crater with high ribbed sides (a single one is shown among the limpets in plate 11). Barnacles remain tightly closed during the tide ebb to keep themselves from drying up, but come to life when the waves sweep high. Then you can see their armored plates open and their feathery legs sweep the water, like the nets of tiny fishermen, to bring into their mouths the plankton of the sea. If you study them carefully enough, you will realize that they are not shellfish at all, but cousins to the shrimp and the crab.

The limpets (plates 10 and 11) cover the rocks of the shore in enormous numbers; they are such staid little homebodies that each one rarely wanders more than a few yards from its home base. Crawling slowly over the rocks when the tide is in, it scrapes off bits of algae with its filelike tongue, then comes back to the same old scar on the rock where it has rested for most of its life. How each limpet finds its way back to its own particular place, when it has no eyes to see, is one of those mysteries of nature which makes the study of sea life so interesting.

Try to pull a limpet off a rock: unless you are lucky enough to catch it unawares, you are in for a struggle. Some of them are capable of holding onto a rock against a seventy pound pull. Imagine, if you can, a human capable of lifting a ten ton truck with one hand, and you get an idea of the relative strength of a limpet!

You can usually tell where a limpet likes to live by the shape of its shell. Both of the limpets shown in plates 10 and 11 are inhabitants of the high tide zone on the protected rocky shores, because the high-peaked top of the ribbed limpet (*Collisella digitalis*) (plate 10) and the uneven ridges of the rough limpet (*Collisella scabra*) (plate 11) are adapted to

-10- Ribbed limpets (189), *Collisella digitalis*

-11- Rough limpets (189), *Collisella scabra*

-12- Blue top snail (204), *Calliostoma ligatum*

comparatively calm waters; they could not stand the surf on exposed rocks where the waves would quickly grab them and sweep them into the depths. On the other hand, the gigantic (often three inches long) owl limpet (*Lottia gigantea*) is so flat and so firmly attached to its "home scar" that waves cannot rip it loose. It is well adapted for living on the outer, surf-swept rocks.

Other limpets are characterized by the living things on which they live. Thus, the surfgrass, or chaffy, limpet (*Notoacmea paleacea*) is narrow in shape and adapted for living on the narrow strands of surfgrass. The small black turban limpet (*Collisella asmi*) lives on the shells of black or brown turban snails (*Tegula funebralis* and *T. brunnea*), while the seaweed limpet (*Notoacmea insessa*) has a translucent brown shell, which makes it look like part of the brown stem of the feather boa kelp (*Egregia menziesii*) on which its lives. The convex-sloped but highly variable shield limpet (*Collisella pelta*) is common in mussel beds, but also often found on various brown algae, such as the surf-loving sea palm (*Postelsia*) (plate 40), where it clings like a boy on a wild swing when the surf whips it back and forth.

The shell of the blue top snail (*Calliostoma ligatum*) (plate 12) is one of a number of prettily ringed top shells found along our coast at low tide. Brown in color, it has a bluish pearly layer just below the surface that becomes visible when the shell becomes worn. The rings on a shell are growth rings, but it is not easy, except for an expert, to judge exactly how old a shell is by its rings. Look closely and you will notice that there are four sets of rings on this snail shell, with a deep indentation between each set. These indicate the inward channels or passageways of the shell and, if you were able to take the snail out of its shell, you would find its body coiled to fit these channels, with the small pointed end up at the top of the shell, where both shell and animal began their growth. An even more attractive top shell, found on exposed rocks at low tide, belongs to the purple-ringed top snail (*Calliostoma annulatum*), which has a beautiful yellow shell with a purple band at the suture.

The upper two of the four animals shown on page 24 belong to the class Gastropoda, which includes snails, limpets, abalones, and nudibranches, and the lower two belong to the class Polyplacophora, the chitons. Both classes belong to the phylum Mollusca (shellfish). They have in common the large, single foot used for moving and for clinging to a surface, and the radula, or filelike tongue, used in feeding, but otherwise they are quite different. The gastropods have a single shell, while the chitons have a series of eight overlapping plates. Scientists consider chitons a more primitive type of mollusca, possibly like the original ancestor of all mollusca. Though primitive, they have fine protection from becoming dried up or washed away by waves, due to their tough shells and powerful suction. However, gastropods are a good deal more numerous and more maneuverable.

Plate 13 shows some of the very common black turban snails (*Tegula funebralis*), which often gather in masses in crevices or on boulders in the middle tide zone. They often blend so successfully with the colors of the darker seaweeds that even large groups of them may be hard to see on the rocks. You will observe on the lower turban snail a black turban limpet (*Collisella asmi*), which gets a free ride wherever the turban goes and undoubtedly finds enough green algae growing on the larger snail's sides to keep it alive. This cleaning may benefit the turban, and both animals get on well together; this is called commensalism, a form of partnership. Another commensal snail that is commonly found on turban snails is the hooked slipper snail (*Crepidula adunca*), which, indeed, looks just like a dark brown slipper with a sharply recurved hook end. In the spring, if you carry a powerful enough magnifying glass, you may see an extraordinary sight through the walls of the transparent egg packs of these tiny snails: the little new born embryos whirling around like dervishes.

Another turban snail, but one that is much more common in the low tide zone from Cape Argo, Oregon, south is the brown turban snail (*Tegula brunnea*), which often swarms in the lower tidepools. It is less often seen than its darker cousin, the black turban, because it hides or travels about under the rockweeds, especially the brown varieties with which its color blends in perfect camouflage.

The lovely red abalone (*Haliotis rufescens*) (plate 14) of the low tide zone is a joy to the many people who hunt it for its delicate and tasty flesh. Though it can grow to the great size of twelve inches, such giants are rarely found, even in the lowest of low tides. Those who hunt it are numerous, and all above seven inches long (the smallest size that can be legally caught) are grabbed quickly by eager seekers. Like most abalones, the red abalone likes to live under overhanging rocks in deep crevices or channels where the tide

-13- Black turban snails (206), *Tegula funebralis*

-14- Red abalone (183), *Haliotis rufescens,* with sea sac rockweed (28), and strands of eelgrass

-15- Mossy chiton (170), *Mopalia muscosa*

-16- Underside of a giant chiton (175), Cryptochiton stelleri

sweeps through. If you try to pry it off, unless you act quickly when it is unaware, you may find your fingers painfully pinched to the rock, possibly losing skin and even flesh before you get them free. I suggest that it is more fascinating and profitable to sit by a deep rock channel at low ebb tide, watching this strange creature move slowly over the rock on its enormous foot as it attacks the rockweed jungle and gobbles up into its large stomach various kinds of brown seaweed. Shown with the abalone are some strands of eelgrass (Zostera) and the fruiting bodies of a sea sac (Halosaccion). If you watch closely some sunny spring day at low tide, you might see this abalone shoot out white clouds of sperm, if a male, or grayish green clouds of eggs, if a female. When the females become fertile they may populate the waters with from 100,000 to two and a half million new little abalones, of which only a handful live to adulthood.

The smaller green abalone (Haliotis fulgens) is common to southern California; the black abalone (Haliotis cracherodii) of the central and northern California coasts is a rugged individualist, able to withstand the rush of the great waves on the outer rocks.

Many exquisitely beautiful or exotic-looking chitons are found along the coast. Most are light-sensitive and seek hiding places under rocks or in dark crevices from the middle to the low tide zone. They are hard to pull from the rocks, clinging almost with the fervor of an abalone, but once pulled off, the eight plates on the back allow them to curl into a defensive circle, very much like a pill bug. Seeking them is like looking for lost treasure, for you must peer under jungles of rockweed, peek into little caves or crevices, and roll over large rocks before—Eureka!—there you see one of these lovely gems of green, lavender, orange, or blue. If you could watch it for many hours, you would see it move slowly over the rocks, scraping off plant food with its filelike radula, or you might see a female, stimulated by the presence of a male, extrude long, jellylike threads of eggs into the water to be fertilized by free-swimming sperm. Most chitons shed their eggs freely.

Plate 15 shows the mossy chiton (Mopalia muscosa), which doesn't mind daylight as much as the other chitons do. Noted for the furry covering of its mantle, this creature likes the walls of caves and comes out on open rocks usually on foggy days. It is common in the low tide zone.

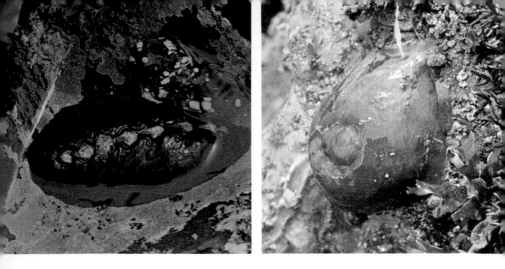

Page 26
   -17- Black chiton (174), *Katharina tunicata*
   -18- Red and green anemone (61), *Tealia crassicornis*
   -19- Map rocks with sandy anemone (64), *Anthopleura elegantissima), and mossy chiton (170)*

Page 28, 29
   -20- Tidepool life

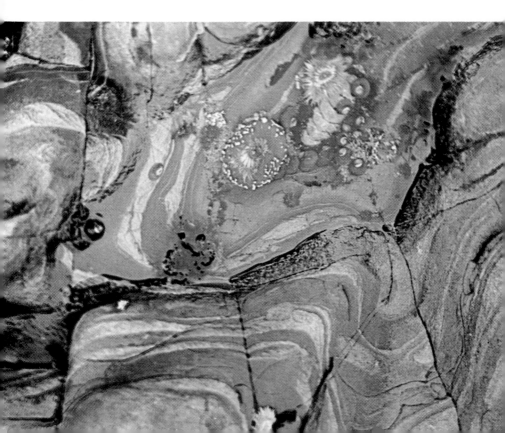

The most extraordinary of all chitons is the giant, or "gumboot," chiton (*Cryptochiton stelleri*). It is the largest of the chitons, sometimes being longer than thirteen inches. The one shown in plate 16 has been photographed upside down to show its enormous foot. The brick red mantle that can be seen around the edges is so extensive that it completely covers the eight plates of the upper side. Many people who find this queer creature are completely unaware that it is a chiton at all. It, too, hunts for plant food mainly at night or on foggy days, and hides among the rockweeds, where its color helps camouflage it. In about a quarter of the specimens encountered, a commensal scale worm (*Arctonoe vittata*) may be found clinging along the edge of the foot under the mantle. The dark hole at one end of the foot is the mouth, from which it is possible to pull the peculiar filelike tongue with a pair of forceps.

Colors are important in identifying many chitons, such as the black chiton (*Katharina tunicata*) shown in plate 17. Some are truly gems, such as the green marbled chiton (*Stenoplax heathiana*), which can be found hidden under rocks in the low tide zone pools or under masses of rockweed, where it avoids both light and potential enemies.

Beauty can be found not only in the fascinating and marvelously varied life on our coasts, but also in the fantastic colors and designs of the rocks on which the life lives. Plate 19 resembles the strange map of an unknown land, where gray rivers meander and twist in extraordinary profusion beneath yellow and orange bluffs, while a mossy chiton (*Mopalia muscosa*) looks like a kind of gray-shingled building in the upper right, its roof carrying queer circular towers that are actually black turban snails. On two sides of it are what appear to be bomb bursts, but are really one expanded and one unexpanded sandy sea anemone (*Anthopleura elegantissima*). Most of this "map" was caused by the twisting of colored sandstone long ago, moved by ancient tectonic forces.

The sandy sea anemone (also shown in plate 50) is generally found in thick clusters on the exposed sides of rocks in the middle tide zone. It uses sand to cover itself, both as protection against drying up and as camouflage from its enemies and the tiny creatures it preys on, such as marine isopods and tiny fish swept near by wave and tide. All anemones have numerous tentacles covered with tiny stinging hairs with which they paralyze their prey. Unwary human

visitors do not have to worry about the stings, but may sit down on what looks like a perfectly innocent bit of sandstone rock only to find themselves sitting on a squishy mess of sea anemones, all squirting protestingly at once!

The red and green anemone (*Tealia crassicornis*) (plate 18) depends not on sand but on its contrasting bright colors for camouflage; these merge with the bright-colored seaweeds of pools and rocks in the low tide zone. The anemone has closed its opening and drawn in its fringe of tentacles in the stance that it usually takes when it considers itself in danger, or has just captured some small prey and has drawn the creature inside to be digested. Most anemones have such powerful digestion that they are able to swallow a crab and then toss out its disgorged and stripped shell fifteen minutes later with every scrap of meat completely digested! That is like a man digesting one complete chicken in the same short time.

Few objects so draw the eyes or fill the mind with speculation as the sight of a giant green anemone (*Anthopleura xanthogrammica*), shown in the color centerpiece, plate 20 on pages 28 and 29. It is sometimes as wide as ten or even twelve inches across, opening its mouthlike maw and waving its numerous green tentacles in the clear water of a large tidepool. To the inexperienced observer it may appear capable of some kind of horrendous deviltry, and the youngster who puts his or her hand down through the water and touches what looks like a twisting mass of green worms is brave indeed. However, the reality differs from appearances. Although touching those tentacles on a very large anemone might give you a tingling sensation, as hundreds of tiny nematocysts, or stinging hairs, reacted to your hand, unless you were especially allergic, it would do you no more harm than would putting your hand into the warm suds of a dishpan.

The common seastar, another frequently found denizen of the tidepool, is also shown in this picture. The seastar is a moving carnivore, while the giant green anemone is a stationary carnivore. The latter often has an enemy hidden about the bases of its tentacles: the sea spider (*Pycnogonum*) lurks there to feed upon its host.

It is impossible to show a complete picture of a tidepool, although we have tried to in our centerpiece, because the whole pool is lined with innumerable hiding places. Varied and interesting creatures find homes and camouflage in these places, which aid in disguising them from our gaze.

Everyone should have the opportunity to experience first-hand the feeling a tidepool can give: a feeling of utter peace and quiet in which, between the rhythmic motion of the waves, the little pool lies still like a crystal drop suspended in space, all life within it seeming to wait with baited breath. Then, the next wave begins to come, first with only a little whispering movement from the sea and a slight waving of seaweed fronds, then with a rush and a heave and a whirling of waters, or with the curl and lift of white foam as a breaker rises over the nearest rock barrier and crashes into the pool. Suddenly the once clear water is murky with bubbles, and seaweed glistens wetly in the sunlight, streaming and twisting into the middle of the pool. The tentacles of the giant green anemones move in an eager and voracious search for food brought by the sea. Look closely down into the swirling waters and you may see the California mussels (*Mytilus californianus*) gaping open their double shells, so that they too can partake of the dinner brought into the pool from the foaming sea; while the great clusters of acorn barnacles (*Balanus*) open up their infolded plates and let loose the intricate nets of their lovely legs. Stirred by the wave, other life too makes its moves in and out of hiding places under the fronds of the seaweed or from rock crevices. Shrimps and tidepool fish may flash out like tiny rockets to seize some luckless creature smaller even than themselves, or you may glimpse for a moment the snakelike form of a large worm, poking up from amidst the mussel jungle.

The mystery and romance of the seashore is perhaps exemplified best by the sea urchins, which dwell in the low tidepools or make their colonies along ridges of rocks that point their fingers into the sea. As the deep boom of the surf sounds hollowly behind a great rock, try sitting safe in the rock's protection and gazing at the life that lines a low tidepool; you may then see the large red sea urchin (*Strongylocentrotus franciscanus*) (plate 21). It is surely utterly different from any animal of the land, for even the porcupine, which bears it some resemblance, has four feet, eyes, and a nose, while this red or red-purple creature looks like a moving, round ball covered with spines. It moves slowly over rock surfaces with its spines, searching for rockweed which it digests in an extraordinarily long digestive tube, which is coiled round and round in its body. On its lower surface, if you turn it over, you will find the equally extraordinary mouth, called "Aristotle's lantern" because its five chisel-like teeth combine with the strong bony plates from which they project to make a structure similar in appearance to an ancient Greek lantern.

The sea urchin is like a seastar that has coiled its five arms into a perfect ball and then somehow sealed up the openings. Like its cousin, the seastar, it has radial water-vascular canals inside its body, extending in five directions, and has three similar projecting appendages: spines, tube feet, and pedicellariae (which have three little biting jaws). On the seastar, the tube feet cover the whole underside of the body, acting for both locomotion and anchoring, and are more conspicuous than on the sea urchin, whose spines cover its test (or shell) like a veritable forest. Only when you look down to the roots of this forest do you find the tube feet poking out here and there through holes in the test. The pedicellariae are still smaller and harder to see, but they also are found on the test under the spines. Push a sharp point against the test, and the spines will come together to fight off the point; push your finger on the spines, and they will move aside. If you push your finger in as far as you can, you may feel the little biting jaws of the pedicellariae taking up the fight as the animal tries to ward off your attack. Each pedicellariae contains a small amount of poison that a smaller creature would feel strongly, but all you will feel is a tingling sensation. Seastars, the principal enemies of the sea urchin, are resisted by these weapons, but seastars keep trying until they can wrap their arms around a sea urchin, break through the armor of the test, and get to the animal inside.

While the red sea urchin may grow to be larger than seven inches wide, its relative, the purple sea urchin (*Strongylocentrotus purpuratus*), rarely becomes more than three inches across (plate 22). Its smaller size is probably due to the fact that the purple urchin is most common on the outer rocks, where the power of the surf is strongest. Here its small size gives the waves less to grab hold of. But its most lasting method of defense against wave power is its ability to wear a hole in a rock into which it can put its body and then cling to it with its spines. A controversy once raged as to how it could dig these holes in hard rock, but most marine biologists now agree that it simply patiently works its spines back and forth like sandpaper against the rock, starting where waves have already worn a depression, and keep-

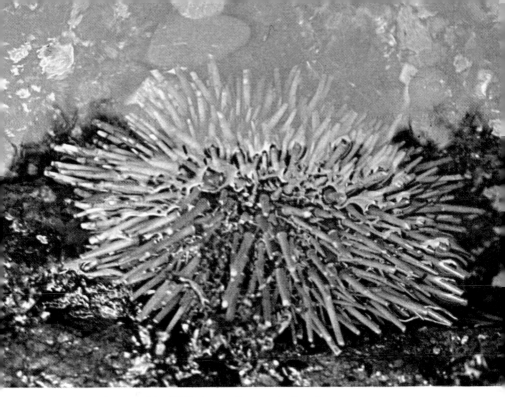

-21- Red sea urchin (300), *Strongylocentrotus franciscanus*
-22- Colony of purple sea urchins (301), *Strongylocentrotus purpuratus*
-23- Red-gilled white-tubed worm (96), *Serpula vermicularis*

-24- Army of ochre seastars (277), *Pisaster ochraceus,* invading a bed of California mussels (248), *Mytilus californianus*

-25- Mussel worm (97), *Nereis vexillosa*

-26- Pink short-spined seastar (280), *Pisaster brevispinus*

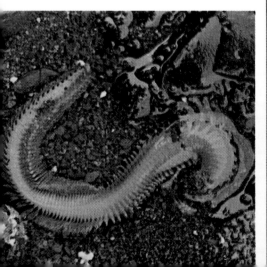

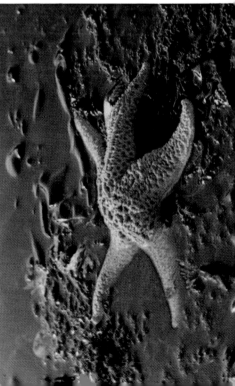

ing on until a satisfactory hole is dug. Some even trap themselves in their holes by growing too big to get out through the original entrance! Such animals cannot go hunting for food, but let the tide bring it to them.

The green sea urchin (*Strongylocentrotus droebachiensis*) lives in sheltered waters mainly from Washington north and is about three inches wide. All three urchins usually carry the flatworm *Syndesmis franciscana* in their intestines, which is about a quarter-inch long; these may or may not harm their hosts. The tiny isopod, *Colidotea rostrata*, is normally only found clinging to the spines of sea urchins.

Worms of many kinds are extremely numerous along our ocean shores, but are often not noticed because of their many methods of hiding or of disguising themselves. Tube worms, for example, may be all but invisible when concealed under rockweed and other life on the rocks. The red-gilled, white-tubed worm, *Serpula vermicularis*, shown in plate 23, is often found in the low tidepools covering the undersurfaces and sides of rocks with its tiny white calcareous tubes. When the tide is in and the worms are undisturbed, their gills make little dots of brilliant carmine on the rock sides, each set of gills waving gently in the water, searching for the microscopic plankton brought in by the waves. The flesh-colored or brown, hairy-headed terebellid worm, *Thelepus crispus*, usually builds parchmentlike tubes in the mud and sand between and under rocks at the bottom of tidepools. All these tube worms protect themselves from their enemies and from drying out when the tide is down by staying in their tubes. They show the often extraordinary beauty of their gills, in colors of red, yellow, and orange, whenever they feel safe and when the tide is bringing in their twice daily meals of plankton from the deep sea.

The mussel worm (*Nereis vexillosa*) shown in plate 25 is writhing in protest against being exposed to an unnatural environment of sunlight and air. The quickest way to find it is to investigate the narrow spaces between the mussels in a mussel colony (plate 24), where the worm finds protection against both waves and enemies. When you pull it out of one of its hiding places, however, your original valor may turn to fear and revulsion because its numerous legs and black, sharp jaws give the impression of something fearsome. Although a big one (they grow from two to twelve inches long) could give you a sharp pinch, most of the fear is ill-founded; instead try observing with pleasure its marvelously iridescent, greenish brown body and its method of slipping quickly through the mussel jungle like a great snake.

The mussel worm is the reputed tiger of this underworld, hunting and killing other creatures there, such as the common scale worm (*Halosydna brevisetosa*); the porcelain crab (*Petrolisthes*) (plate 35); the dark-backed isopod (*Cirolana harfordi*); the mussel ribbon worm (*Emplectonema gracile*), which forms tangles of what look like tiny rubber bands among the mussels; and the tiny mussel bed sand flea (*Elasmopus rapax*).

The seastar, of numerous species, is another common carnivore of the rocky beaches, traveling about over the rocks attacking mussels, snails, sea urchins, and other creatures, not by the sudden leap of a tiger, but by slowly moving up on these almost stationary creatures and then wrapping itself around them, somewhat like a boa constrictor. But the seastar, unlike the snake, is dealing with mainly armored prey, and its attack must somehow get inside the shell to be effective. This it does by grasping the shell firmly with its tube feet, then exerting an overwhelming pressure with its muscular arms until something gives way, and the shell is broken open. Then it protrudes its stomach out of its body, enfolds the living animal, and digests it outside of its own body! Besides the tube feet with which it moves and holds on, each of which is furnished with a small suction cup at the end, the seastar also has pedicellariae, which it uses to keep its surface clean of algae or barnacles, or sometimes for catching small creatures to eat. Many have very tough skins which protect them well from most enemies and from the surf.

The ochre seastar (*Pisaster ochraceus*), also known as the common seastar sometimes moves in numbers, like an advancing army, into cities of mussels, storming the outer walls (shells) of these fortified places (plate 24), and tearing open the shells of the unfortunate ones on the outer fringes.

The pink short-spined seastar (*Pisaster brevispinus*) (plate 26) is usually found only in quiet waters or deep down below low tide level on the more open coasts. However, it is very common in Puget Sound and distinguished there by its often gigantic size (sometimes more than two feet in diameter). It cannot be preserved by drying as can the common seastar, since its body is so much softer. It soon collapses on exposure to the air.

-27- Delicate six-rayed seastar (281), *Leptasterias pusilla,* and girl

-28- Sunflower star (289), *Pycnopodia helianthoides*
-29- Snaky-armed brittle star (293), *Amphiodia occidentalis*

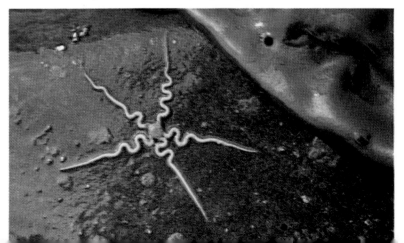

The little girl in plate 27 is looking at one of the delicate six-rayed seastars (*Leptasterias pusilla*), an example of life that is exceedingly common, but not often seen; these little fellows (less than one inch wide) hide by day under the seaweed in the middle tide zone pools. Their larger, six-rayed cousins, *Leptasterias hexactis*, with broader rays and twice the diameter, live mainly in the same kind of hiding places in the low tide zone, but prefer stronger surf.

Night is a special time to explore the beaches, when many creatures come out from their hiding places. Standing still on a rocky reef at low tide on a dark night, you are almost certain to hear the sounds and sense the presence of many kinds of living things filling the darkness with movement. Turn on your light, and suddenly you will see dark forms scuttling, eyes glittering, and brightly colored creatures moving slowly over the tops of the rocks.

Come when the tide is out to one of the deep tidepools at the very edge of the retreating sea, and if you are lucky, you may see a glory of glories moving below you in the crystal clear waters. It is like a bursting vision of the sun itself, caught in the waters, and bears the appropriate name of Sunflower Star (*Pycnopodia helianthoides*). It is a creature so delicately lovely and symmetrical (see plate 28) that you will scarcely believe your eyes. With the softest skin of all the starfish, the greatest number of arms (up to twenty-four), and the biggest size (sometimes over two feet wide), it is indeed a marvelous treasure, the loveliest flower of our tidepools. It holds still another distinction as the fastest moving of all seastars. Its many arms pulsate, flow, lift, and push down in what amounts to a rhythmic dance as it moves across the bottom of a pool. But taken out, it crumbles, shrinks, and dies very quickly, so it is best to leave it alone for others to enjoy.

A large book could be written about the under-rock life in the tidepools, but described here are a few of the more fantastic and interesting things to be seen. One strange form of life is the snaky-armed brittle star (*Amphiodia occidentalis*) (plate 29), which hides in the sandy mud under large rocks and must be searched for in pockets where the bottom oozes softly beneath your fingers. Be careful in handling it, for its arms break easily.

Of the tidepool animals, crabs probably are the noisiest and the most pushy. When you come out along a rock reef, you hear them scuttling before you; they make no noise with their mouths, only sometimes a soft bubbling. They scrape and rustle against the rocks in a widespread, whispering movement of life. If you sit still, they soon come out from their hiding places in the cracks and crannies, especially if the day is foggy or at dawn or evening, and walk sideways with an absurd dignity, their long-stalked eyes peering up myopically, like so many self-important old dignitaries going to a city council meeting. Most of them are scavengers of dead and dying life on the beach, and are not above dropping all dignity to fight, like a herd of hungry pigs, over bits of offal they find, their armored claws clattering and snapping against each other.

The crab you are most likely to see first is the little, lined shore crab (*Pachygrapsus crassipes*) (plate 30), which is rarely over two inches wide, and which is just as likely to lift up lively pincers and try to fight you as to scuttle away in fright under some rock. These crabs are found under nearly every loose rock or in every crevice and cave of the high tide zone; they certainly know how to make a living, or there wouldn't be so many of them! The crab in plate 30 is green, but some are dark red as well.

As you move deeper into the middle tide zone, the lined shore crab is gradually supplanted by the larger purple shore crab (*Hemigrapsus nudus*) (plate 31), which is less a rock-hiding crab than a rockweed-hiding crab, and just as numerous in the thick foliage of the middle zone as the other crab is among the more barren rocks higher up. *Hemigrapsus* may be less evident, mainly because it has better places in which to hide. The picture shows it standing on the sea lettuce (*Ulva*) that often shelters it. The purple spots on the white undersides of its claws are distinctive. It can also put up a good fight and, since a crab's claws are at least forty times as strong as a man's hand in proportion to size, look out!

The common hermit crab (*Pagurus*), shown resting in a black turban snail shell in plate 32, is just as pugnacious as the other crabs, but even more comical. A hermit crab's life is a series of hunts for empty snail shells, mainly the turban's, for as the crab grows, it must move into new homes. At this task, as well as at fighting among themselves over food and females, hermit crabs are accomplished, if unconscious, clowns. When the crab is house hunting, every new empty shell encountered is approached with the seriousness of a customs inspector checking over a bag full of valuable dia-

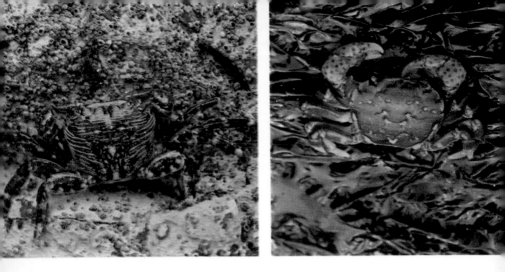

Page 40
-30- Lined shore crab (150), *Pachygrapsus crassipes*
-31- Purple shore crab (151), *Hemigrapsus nudus*
-32- Hermit crab (145), *Pagurus,* in black turban shell
-33- Red-spotted cancer crab (147), *Cancer attennarius,* on violet
   rockweed (29), *Cryptopleura violaceae*

Page 41
-34- Shield-backed kelp crab (155), *Pugettia producta,* (upperside)
-35- Thick-clawed porcelain crab (138), *Pachycheles rudis*
-36- Shield-backed kelp crab (155), *Pugettia producta,* (underside)

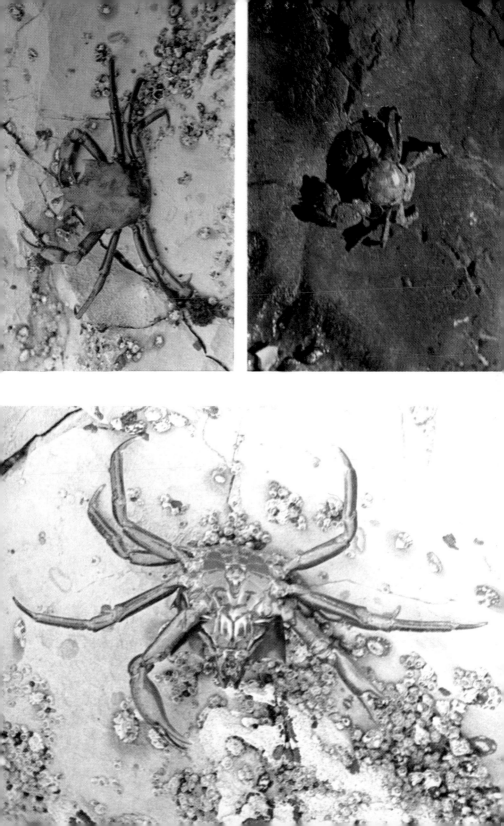

monds. The shell is inspected and rotated, and its entrance way is explored with sensitive antennae that seem to tell the crab, within a fraction, whether this is the ideal home for it. Then—Pop! Pop!—out of one shell it darts, whirls in a flash, and plunges backward into the other shell so fast that your eyes can scarcely follow it. At fighting, hermit crabs display a great deal of enthusiasm but little science, something like a pair of amateur pillow fighters producing a lot of sweat but no blood.

Down in the large low tidepools the red-spotted cancer crab (Cancer attennarius) is probably king, unless its big brothers, the common edible crab (Cancer magister) or the red cancer crab (Cancer productus) come up from the lower depths to take over. In plate 33, attennarius is resting on the fronds of a violet rockweed (Cryptopleura violaceae). Like magister, which may reach up to nine inches in diameter, attennarius also has edible flesh, but its smaller size (generally under five inches) makes it less sought-out. The rarer Cancer productus, which is slightly larger than attennarius, is sometimes found here too.

Both the upperside and the underside of the common shield-backed kelp crab (Pugettia producta) are shown in plates 34 and 36 to illustrate how the bright red of its underside contrasts with the more somber and camouflaging olive brown of its upperside. Hidden among the dark fronds of such rockweeds as Egregia, Laminaria, and Porphyra, it is often very difficult to see, and has the further drawback of being better found with the hands than with the eyes! A large three-inch-wide one is so agile at pinching with its claws that one carelessly brushed is certain to draw blood. Sharp spines on its legs help this crab cling to its protecting seaweed. The graceful kelp crab (Pugettia gracilis) is found in more quiet waters, especially in Washington and Oregon, while the southern kelp crab (Taliepus nuttallii), which is often blotched with light colors on purple, is the common form in southern California.

Shown in plate 35 is the thick-clawed porcelain crab (Pachycheles rudis), commonly found on wharf pilings. It looks very much like the flat porcelain crab (Petrolisthes cinctipes), but has conspicuous granules on its large front claws. Both rarely get to be more than one-half inch in width, but their beautiful reddish brown to brown carapaces make them exciting to find. When their rock is turned over these small, flat crabs scuttle about excitedly, looking for new cover; do them the kindness of turning the rock back over when you have finished looking at them. They have an interesting way of preventing capture by suddenly throwing off a claw or walking leg whenever they think someone is about to grab them. A large egg mass is often found under the tail plates of a female; these do not hatch into young crabs, but into tiny, transparent zooea, or primary larval forms, which swim freely in the sea as part of the plankton.

The spectacular California sea cucumber (*Parastichopus californicus*) has a dark form that looks almost exactly like the giant chiton (*Cryptochiton*), shown in plate 37. But the chiton shows ridges on its back, indicating the shells hidden under its mantle, while the cucumber is smooth and looks more like a fat sea slug, especially when seen moving wormlike over the rocks. The movements of its body wall are actually caused by the movement of the tube feet on its underside, which are almost identical to the tube feet of the seastar. The tentacles around the mouth of the cucumber are also a modified form of tube feet and help it scrape various organic particles into its mouth as the animal moves along in a deep, very low tidepool. This indicates that the cucumber is related neither to the chiton nor to the sea slug, but to the seastar and sea urchin. Its color is generally black or dark brown, or sometimes dark red or yellow, and the proboscis which extends the mouth is generally reddish. When defending themselves, these large cucumbers call to mind an angry camel or a large, important man bursting with rage. If further annoyed, they actually regurgitate their entire insides in "a most disgusting manner!" If the cucumber is put back into the water and left alone, new insides will soon grow back.

There are many spectacular and interesting tidepool fish, but they are often hard to see, as shown in plate 38, where a convict fish, or painted greenling, (*Oxylebius pictus*) merges its brilliant red and yellowish white colors with the equally bright colors of other tidepool life, such as the delightful club-tipped anemone (*Corynactis californica*), which is seen in the upper part of the picture, the yellowish coralline algae (*Corallina*), and the red sponges (*Ophlitaspongia pennata*), which dot the rock here and there.

Like most tidepool fish, the convict fish darts rapidly for cover under the seaweed when it is disturbed, so it is best to sit quietly by a tidepool for some time patiently waiting until the life within the water is no longer conscious of any disturbing influence. You may then observe other small fish

-37- Giant chiton (176), *Cryptochiton stelleri,* next to feather boa kelp (11) *Egregia menziesii*. Bumps betray shell ridges underneath the mantle

-38- Convict fish (332), *Oxylebius pictus,* club-tipped anemone (59), and red sponges

coming out of hiding to hunt for food in the clear waters or lazily swimming about through the channels between the rockweed. The tidepool sculpin, or rockpool Johnny, and the little clingfish may both be identified by their rather large ugly heads and their quickly tapering bodies. The former have pretty dark saddles on their backs, while the latter have dark mottling against a lighter-colored background. The dark, slender eel-like pricklebacks wriggle violently under rocks.

Plate 39 shows another of those little spots of wonder caused by the combination of life and rock in pleasing motifs, like the imaginary map shown in plate 19. This is a different, yet equally beautiful, miniature landscape: splotches of orange sponge (*Ophlitaspongia pennata*) and touches of green rockweed look like the trees and beaches of a south sea island, with surrounding and protecting reefs lapped by the blue-gray waters of the South Pacific.

This chapter can hardly end with a more exciting and spectacular view than that in plate 40: sea palms (*Postelsia palmaeformis*) bow to wave shock on one of the outer ledges, as the swells of six thousand miles of ocean reach their end. These "palms" (also shown in plate 42), actually only a form of seaweed, appear so like their namesakes that anyone who has been in a typhoon in the South Pacific will be swept again with the feelings of dread that come when 130-mile-an-hour winds sweep huge waves over a tropical island. One can almost see the tiny figures of men, women, and children lashed helplessly to the trunks of the palms.

Just as the real palms of the South Seas owe their lives to their ability to bend and give before the wind and water of great storms, so the sea palms survive on the outermost rocks by bending and twisting even more before the impact of the mighty waves. Animals such as the sometimes brown and white-rayed shield limpets (*Collisella pelta*), described earlier, have found the stems of the sea palm good places on which to live, for the give of the sea palms protects the animals on the plants from the full force of the wave shock. The sea palms do not have true roots, stems, or leaves like the palm tree, but their holdfasts, which are made up of numerous small fibers, are so able to cling to the surface of the rocks that the largest waves rarely tear them loose. Such life is an example of how plants can adapt themselves to truly harsh conditions.

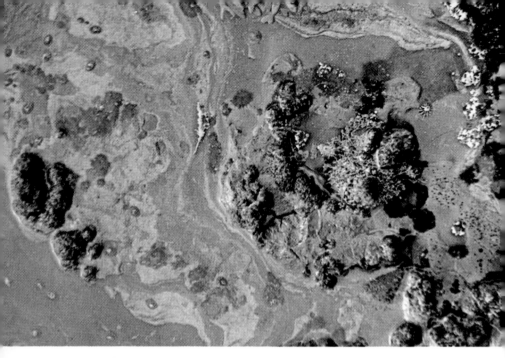

-39- Velvety red sponge (42) (orange colored in this photo), *Ophlitaspongia pennata,* and peculiarly-marked rocks

-40- Sea palms (12), *Postelsia palmaeformis,* in surf

Systematic List of Plants and Animals

The following list of brief descriptions of plants and animals found in or near tidepools include most of the common and important species from Alaska to northern Baja California. Since this list includes mainly plants and animals of the tidepools of the rocky coasts, species found on the sandy beaches and mud flats are rarely included. But the tidepools of the rocky coasts possess more species by far, as well as the most colorful and interesting ones. Many of these species are also commonly found on the rocky shores of bays and estuaries, where they are usually completely protected from surf.

This list of descriptions and the illustrations and color plates will help give you an overall picture of the life of the shores. Each species is arranged by its place in the plant and animal kingdoms, and the zones or habitats where each can most commonly be found are also listed. Often, even if you cannot identify a plant or animal you find down to the exact species, you should still be able to find where it belongs in relation to phylum, class, order, family, or genus. Since common names of seashore plants and animals are often lacking in the literature, we have tried to remedy this in this book by giving common names to those species still not named in other books, based on specific characteristics that help to identify them. Even if these new names do not come into common usage, they will at least help with identification. Good common names are a form of folklore that take time to achieve general acceptance.

Abbreviation Key

SPLZ = Splash zone
HTZ = High tide zone
MTZ = Middle tide zone
LTZ = Low tide zone
OR = Outer rocks with strong surf
IR = Inner rocks with less surf and protective shores
-1-, -2-, etc. = number of the color plate of a species

41. Sea lettuce,
    Ulva sp.

42. Sea palms,
    Postelsia palmaeformis

43. Purple sponge,
    Haliclona sp.

44. Ostrich-plume hydroid,
    Aglaophenia latirostris

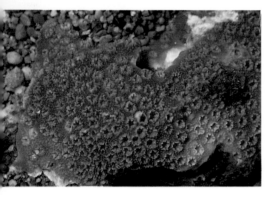

45. Purple hydrocoral,
    Allopora porphyra

46. Purple sail jellyfish,
    Velella velella

47. Club-tipped anemone,
Corynactis californica

48. Proliferating anemone,
Epiactis prolifera

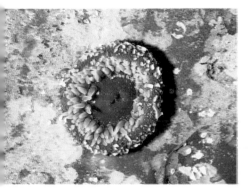

49. Strawberry anemone,
Tealia lofotenis

50. Sandy anemone,
Anthopleura elegantissima

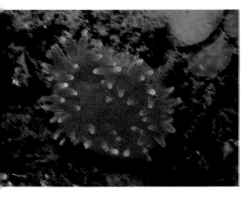

51. Orange-cup coral,
Balanophyllia elegans

52. Twisted brown ribbon worm,
Amphiporus bimaculatus

53. Feather-duster worm,
    Eudistylia polymorpha

54. Goose-neck barnacle,
    Pollicipes polymerus

55. Western sea roach,
    Ligia occidentalis

56. Bay ghost shrimp,
    Callianassa californiensis

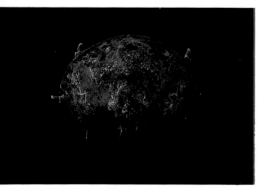

57. Umbrella-backed crab,
    Cryptolithodes sitchensis

58. Lined chiton,
    Tonicella lineata

59. Rough keyhole limpet,
Diodora aspera

60. Owl limpet,
Lottia gigantea

61. Monterey dorid,
Archidoris montereyensis

62. Hopkin's rose,
Hopkinsia rosacea

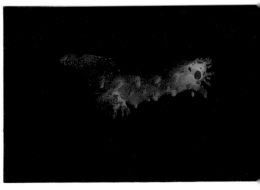

63. Ring-spotted dorid,
Diaulula sandiegensis

64. Sea-clown nudibranch,
Triopha catalinae

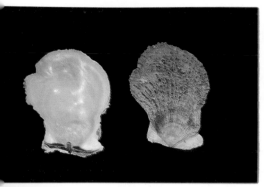

65. Giant rock scallop,
    Hinnites giganteus

66. Red seastar,
    Henricia leviuscula

67. Stiff-footed sea cucumber,
    Eupentacta quinquesemita

68. California sea cucumber,
    Parastichopus californicus

69. Brilliant red hide tunicate,
    Cnemidocarpa finmarkiensis

70. Gold garibaldi,
    Hypsypops rubicunda

Common Seashore Plants

Division Chlorophyta—Green algae or seaweeds
Class Chlorophytaeae
Order Ulotrichales
Family Ulvaceae—Sea lettuce and sea felt

1. Yellow-Green Hairweed, *Enteromorpha intestinalis.* -5- Species vary greatly in size, the branches sometimes being 1 m (39") long; in other plants, especially in the Monterey Peninsula, not more than 20 cm (8"). Color yellow-green to grass green, with blades frequently compressed and contorted. Usually hollow at base of leaflike stem. Alaska to Baja. SPLZ, HTZ, IR.

2. Proliferating Hairweed, *Enteromorpha prolifera.* Many very narrow, tubular stems arise from one base, 4-6 cm (1½-2¼") tall; dark green to golden green. Alaska to Baja. HTZ, MTZ, IR.

3. Common Sea Lettuce, *Ulva lactuca.* -41- Blades thin and broad, up to 30 cm (12") long and not over 4 times the width; sometimes spirally twisted or densely ruffled, but not toothed. Grass-green, becoming brown or black with age. Attached to rocks or other seaweed. Abundant from Alaska to Baja. HTZ to LTZ, IR, OR.

Order Cladophorales
Family Cladophoraceae

4. Green Dome Seaweed, *Cladophora columbiana.* 3-6 cm (1¼-2½") tall. Forms bright green, dome-shaped tufts or cushions on rocks, looking like erect slick green hair. Regularly accumulates sand until it is nearly buried. British Columbia to Baja. MIZ, LIZ.

Order Codiales
Family Codiaceae

5. Spongeweed or **Deadman's Fingers,** *Codium fragile.* 10-30 cm (4-12") high. Dark green to blackish green fingerlike fronds, sometimes with whitish hairs. Erect stems are cylindrical and usually branched; may also form mats; grows on tops or sides of rocks. Alaska to Baja. MTZ, LTZ, IR.

Division Phaeophyta—Brown algae
Class Phaeophyceae
Order Chordariales
Family Ralfsiaceae

6. Tar Spot Alga, *Ralfsia pacifica.* Olive brown to dark brown; upper surface with concentric or radial ridges. All of lower surface attached to rock; from above it looks like a flat, irregular-shaped spot of sticky tar. Alaska to Baja. HTZ, MTZ, IR and OR.

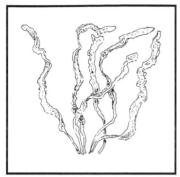

1. *Enteromorpha intestinalis*

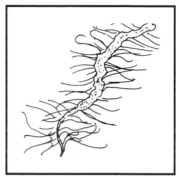

2. *Enteromorpha prolifera*

3. *Ulva lactuca*

4. *Cladophora columbiana*

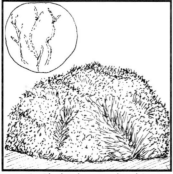

4. *Cladophora columbiana*

5. *Codium fragile*

Family Chordariaceae

7. Thickly Leaved Rockweed, *Analipus japonicus.* Profusely-branched; dark brown to tan; main stems are up to 35 cm (13½") long. Usually many long, slender branches, each thickly covered with "leaves." Often appears draped over rocks when tide is out. Alaska to Pt. Conception, California. MTZ, LTZ, IR and OR.

Order Laminariales
Family Laminariaceae

8. Dense Clumped Laminarian, *Laminaria sinclairii.* Up to 1 m (39") tall; rich dark brown in color. The rhizome (prostrate stem) bears dense clumps of erect, cylindrical stems, each terminating with a long, linear single blade; blades smooth and about twice as long as the stems. British Columbia to Ventura Co., California. On rocks in MTZ and LTZ.

9. Long Bladed Laminarian, *Laminaria farlowii.* Plant with single blade and stem up to 5 m (16') long; dark chocolate brown; blade broadly linear with an irregularly wrinkled and depressed surface. British Columbia to Baja. LTZ, IR, OR.

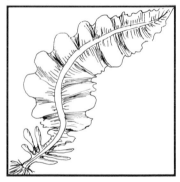

9. Laminaria farlowii   *10. Alaria marginata*

Family Alariaceae

10. Long Bladed Alaria, *Alaria marginata.* Blade 2–6 m (7–20') long, with conspicuous dark midrib, rising from a short stem, and often tattered at the end. General color dark tan, with rows of chocolate brown spots (sporangia) on mature plants. The base is black. Alaska to central California. LTZ, OR.

11. Feather Boa Kelp, *Egregia menziesii.* -4-, -37- Plant 5–15 m (16–49') long, the larger specimens subtidal, chocolate brown to olive green. Stem rises from steady holdfast with several long, flattened branches densely covered with broadly to narrowly spatula-shaped blades; blades up to 8 cm (3") long. Surface of stem and

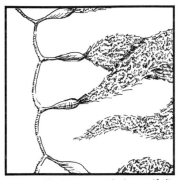 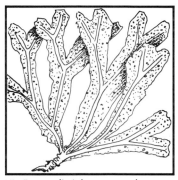

13. *Macrocystis integrifolia*   15. *Fucus distichus ssp. edentatus*

blades often covered with small blunt tubercles. Alaska to Baja. MTZ, LTZ, IR and OR.

Family Lessoniaceae

12. Sea Palm, *Postelsia palmaeformis*. -40-, -42- Up to 60 cm (23½") tall. Golden brown in color, resembling a miniature palm tree bowing to wave shock. Thick stems terminate in ribbonlike blades, these up to 25 cm (10") long. British Columbia to Morro Bay, California. In groups on rocks. HTZ, MTZ, OR.

13. Small Perennial Kelp, *Macrocystis integrifolia*. Up to 6 m (20') long; brown to golden brown; stem dichotomously branched 1–4 times near base; terminal lateral blades rising from pear-shaped bladders up to 40 cm (16") long and 8 cm (3⅛") wide. British Columbia to central California. Normally lives in waters 35–50 feet deep, but also in tidal channels and rocky ledges of the LTZ. IR and OR.

14. Giant Perennial Kelp, *Macrocystis pyrifera*. Differs mainly from *M. integrifolia* in size. Up to 45 m (148') long; terminal lateral blades up to 80 cm (31½") long and 40 cm (16") wide. Alaska to Baja. LTZ and below.

Order Fucales
Family Fucaceae

15. Common Brown Rockweed, *Fucus distichus* ssp. *edentatus*. From 10–30 cm (4–12") tall, or taller; olive brown to dark brown. Has numerous flattened, regularly forked branches and branchlets lying on one plane, with prominent midribs. Fertile and mature plants may have swollen branch tips, covered with tiny pits, which hold male and female gametes. N. Washington to Pt. Conception, California. HTZ, MTZ.

16. Spindle-Shaped Rockweed, *Pelvetia fastigiata*. Up to 90 cm (35") tall. Has many forked stalks, inflated like spindles at ends. Color yellowish brown to greenish olive; several erect stems arise from a holdfast. British Columbia to Baja. HTZ, MTZ, forming beds on rocks somewhat protected from open surf.

16. Pelvetia fastigiata

17. Porphyra perforata

Division Rhodophyta—Red algae
Class Bangiophyceae
Order Bangiales
Family Bangiaceae

17. California Nori or **Purple Laver**, *Porphyra perforata*. Grows in dense groups and varies greatly in size, but can grow up to 150 cm (60") tall; length and width nearly the same; color brownish purple to gray-green. The blade rising from a disk-shaped holdfast has deeply ruffled margins and lobes; beautiful when floating on water. Alaska to Baja. HTZ, MTZ.

Class Florideophyceae
Order Nemaliales
Family Achrochaetiaceae

18. Red-Velvet Rockweed, *Rhodochorton rothii*. Forms an extensive, deep red, and velvety covering on rocks in shaded areas or caves. S. California to Alaska. HTZ.

Order Cryptonemiales
Family Corallinaceae

19. Mauve Coralline Alga, *Lithothamnium pacificum*. Circular or irregular pinkish purple alga on rocks, 10–14 cm (4–5$\frac{1}{2}$") wide. Upper surface of plant body covered with cylindrical outgrowths, 4–6 mm ($\frac{1}{8}$–$\frac{1}{4}$") wide and up to 10 mm ($\frac{2}{5}$") tall. Crusts appear on rocks, seashells, etc., sometimes overlapping. British Columbia to s. California. MTZ, LTZ.

20. Tall Coralline Alga, *Corallina officianalis* var. *chilensis*.

20. Corallina officianalis var. *chilensis*

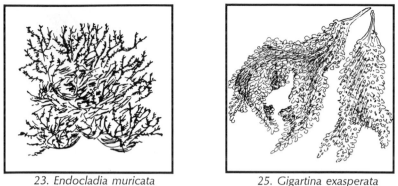

23. *Endocladia muricata*   25. *Gigartina exasperata*

Erect segmented shoots 5–15 cm (2–6") tall, and whitish, pinkish, or purplish. Coral-like in appearance, as are the *Bossiella* (below). Alaska to Chile. On rocks, often in tidepools. Usually LTZ and below.

21. Scarlet Coralline Alga, *Bossiella californica* ssp. *californica*. Erect segmented shoots 4–12 cm (1½–4¾") tall, red-pink; segments sometimes arrowhead-shaped with wings blunt and thick. 2–8 (usually 6) fertile cavities on each segment. Central California to Baja. LTZ.

22. Stout Coralline Alga, *Bossiella plumosa*. Erect segmented shoots 3–7 cm (1⅛–2¾") high, red-purple. Branches opposite at almost every upper axial segment of the plant; segments prominently winged, the wings thin and sharp-edged; usually 2 fertile cavities on each segment. Alaska to Baja. LTZ.

Family Endocladiaceae

23. Wirebrush Alga, *Endocladia muricata*. Plant body 4–8 cm (1½–3") tall; blackish brown to dark red. Densely bushy and with tiny spines that create a harsh-feeling texture; tiny fruit are lighter colored than branches. Alaska to Baja, on tops or vertical faces of rocks. HTZ, OR.

Order Gigartinales
Family Soleriaceae

24. Red Fan-Shaped Seaweed, *Opuntiella californica*. Plant body up to 20 cm (8") tall and 30 cm (12") broad; deep dark red; primary and secondary blades fan-shaped to broadly obovate. Common on rocks exposed to strong surf. Alaska to Baja. LTZ, mostly subtidal.

Family Gigartinaceae

25. Turkish Towel Alga, *Gigartina exasperata*. Blades deep brownish red, usually with irregular margins, up to 90 cm (35") long; usually 2–3 blades 15–30 cm (6–12") wide growing from a single holdfast; short uniform outgrowths on surface give it the texture of a Turkish towel. British Columbia to Baja. Common on all rocky headlands. LTZ and below.

26. Grapestone Seaweed, *Gigartina* sp. -6- All species of *Gigartina* are thickly to sparsely covered with papillate outgrowths that resemble grape seeds. Some species are quite large, up to 38 cm (15") long with blades 15–20 cm (6–8") wide, but most species are much smaller—from 5–13 cm (2–5") long. Margins may be entire, forked, leafy, or irregular. Color varies between species: olive, greenish purple, brownish red, etc. Alaska to Baja. MTZ, LTZ.

27. Iridaea cordata splendens

27. Iridescent Seaweed, *Iridaea cordata* var. *splendens.* -8- From 40–120 cm (16–48") long; blades thick, lanceolate to broadly ovate, margins entire. Makes iridescent dark purplish covers in the tidepools on the long strands. British Columbia to n. Baja. LTZ, OR.

Order Rhodymeniales
Family Rhodymeniaceae

28. Sea Sac, *Halosaccion glandiforme.* -6- Up to 25 cm (10") tall. Yellowish brown to reddish purple in color. Several cylindrical sacs regularly on a single holdfast, sacs filled with water. Alaska to Mexico. HTZ, MTZ on rocks and in clefts.

Order Ceramiales
Family Delesseriaceae

29. Violet Rockweed, *Cryptopleura violaceae.* -33- Purplish olive to greenish pink (most specimens have a greenish tinge); plant body slender, 15–25 cm (6–10") tall, with long, ribbonlike

28. Halosaccion glandiforme

29. Cryptopleura violacea

central blades nearly dichotomously to irregularly forked; margins usually entire. British Columbia to Baja. LTZ, OR.

Family Rhodomelaceae

30. Lavender Alga, *Laurencia pacifica.* 10–25 cm (4–10") tall. Deep reddish purple or bright lavender under water, the branchlets blue-tipped. Erect stems are free and conical, profusely branched; final branches in whorls of 3 or 4. Monterey Peninsula to Baja. LTZ, usually IR.

31. Sea Laurel, *Laurencia spectabilis.* From 15–30 cm (6–12") tall; deep purplish red in color. Smooth, blunt, flattened, cartilaginous branches without midribs are distinctive; lower third of branches undivided. Alaska to San Diego. MTZ, LTZ.

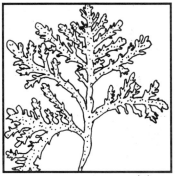

31. Laurencia spectabilis

Division Anthophyta—Flowering plants
Class Monocotyledoneae—Parallel-veined plants
Order Najadales
Family Zosteraceae—Surf and eel grasses

32. Surfgrass, *Phyllospadix* sp. -7- 30–60 cm (1–2') high; rhizomes thick, tuberlike. Green, submerged marine grasses, wiry-compressed, with sheathed, spearlike leaves. Flowers in two-ranked spathes (leaves surrounding flower). MTZ, LTZ, IR, OR.

33. Eelgrass, *Zostera marina.* -14- One to three meters (3–10') long. Branched stems rise from a slender, creeping rhizome; leaves ribbonlike and blunt-ended, in two ranks. Shallow water of bays, estuaries, and mud flats. Occasionally LTZ, IR.

Common Seashore Animals

Phylum Porifera—Sponges

Sponges are recognized by regularly-spaced volcano or craterlike openings called oscula, sometimes rather small to see. They usually have a gritty feel; sometimes dangerous to touch.

34. Vanilla Sponge, *Xestospongia vanilla.* Smooth white crust on undersides of rocks or in crevices; looks like cake frosting. Along the whole coast. LTZ, IR.

35. Stinging Sponge, *Stelletta* sp. White rough crusts on sides of caves that sting like splintered glass when touched. Whole coast. LTZ, IR.

36. Purple Sponge, *Haliclona permollis.* -43- Vivid purple to lavender, soft encrustations on rocks; surface has conspicuous, regular, volcano-like oscula. British Columbia to central California. MTZ, LTZ, IR.

37. Orange Woody Sponge, *Tethya aurantia.* About 8 cm (3") wide. Bright orange or yellow, woody-fibered, hemispherical; often covered with green algae; base has radiating core structure. Whole coast. LTZ, IR.

38. Crumb-Of-Bread Sponge, *Halichondria panicea.* Often forms encrustations on rocks up to 3 cm (1¼") thick. Abundant in some areas, especially north of Point Conception. Orange to green, amorphous, fragile; volcano-like oscula somewhat raised. Whole coast. LTZ, IR.

39. Stinking Sponge, *Lissodendoryx firma.* Clusters up to 8 cm (3") thick; 15 cm (6") in diameter. Lumpy yellow or tan surface, foul smelling. If broken, many small sea creatures may be found living in the cavernous interior. Central California. LTZ, IR.

40. Vermilion-Red Sponge, *Antho lithophoenix.* Soft, vermilion-red, lumpy, almost papillate, surface with very small oscula. Central California. LTZ, IR.

41. Smooth Red Sponge, *Plocamia karykina.* Appears in bright red layers, up to 2 cm (¾") thick. Surface smooth; consistency firm and woody. Comparatively large oscula irregular and far apart. British Columbia to Baja. MTZ, LTZ, IR.

42. Velvety Red Sponge, *Ophlitaspongia pennata.* -39- Flat, encrusting, coral red to orange sponge; openings star-shaped; feels velvety. Most common on vertical rocks shaded from direct sunlight. British Columbia to Baja. MTZ, LTZ, IR.

43. Sharp-Spined Creamy Sponge, *Leucandra heathi.* Globular to pear-shaped, cream-colored colony, up to 9 cm (3½") wide; accommodates its shape to crevices; surface bristly; longer spines protect its large, volcano-like central osculum. Spines crumble easily. British Columbia to Baja. LTZ, IR.

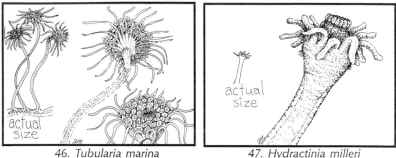

46. *Tubularia marina*

47. *Hydractinia milleri*

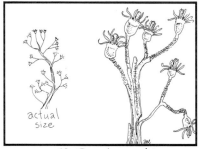

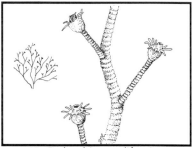

48. *Garveia annulata*

49. *Eudendrium californicum*

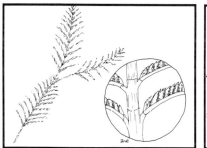

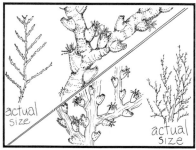

51. *Aglaophenia struthionides*

52. *Abietinaria anguina*
53. *Abietinaria greenii*

44. Urn-Shaped Sponge, *Leucilla nuttingi*. Creamy white; up to 5 cm (2") tall. Usually occurs in clumps of 12 or more suspended under ledges or in crevices. British Columbia to Baja. Very low LTZ, IR.

45. Sulphur Sponge, *Aplysina fistularis*. Clusters vary greatly in size; yellow and coarse-textured, with raised oscula; turns purple or black if removed from the water. Under ledges and on the sides of rocks, making thick mats. Sulphur odor. Whole coast. LTZ, IR.

Phylum Cnidaria—Hydroids, anemones, jellyfish, and corals.

(All cnidarians lack a true head, but usually bear a crown of stinging tentacles around a mouth by which they capture their prey.)

Class Hydrozoa—Hydroids and jellyfish
Order Hydroida
Suborder Anthomedusae

46. Solitary Hydroid, *Tubularia marina*. Bright orange or pink polyps, 3–5 cm (1–2") tall, solitary or in groups of evenly spaced individuals, arise from a stalk that creeps and holds fast to a rock surface. Medusoid heads red with pink centers. Found under ledges or in rocky crevices. Pacific Grove to n. California. LTZ, IR, OR

47. Fuzzy Pink Hydroid, *Hydractinia milleri*. About 4 mm (⅛") high; appears in fuzzy pink patches on the sides of rocks. In a primitive manner, three different zooids (individual organisms in a composite group) separately handle reproduction, nutrition, and defense. Vancouver Island to central California. LTZ, IR.

48. Orange Hydroid, *Garveia annulata*. Colony up to 5 cm (2") tall, with 20–30 zooids. Uniform orange color except for lighter orange tentacles. Hydranths or heads are usually dome-shaped. Alaska to s. California. LTZ, IR.

49. California Stick Hydroid, *Eudendrium californicum*. Colony bushy, up to 15 cm (6") tall. The brown stem, by which the spirally branching colony attaches to a rock, is firm and strong. The zooids look like pink cotton balls, each with a mouth surrounded by threadlike white tentacles, which retract slowly if touched. British Columbia to Monterey Bay, on ledges and in crevices. LTZ, IR.

Suborder Leptomedusae

50. Ostrich-Plume Hydroid, *Aglaophenia latirostris*. -44- Plumes 5–8 cm (2–3") tall, usually arranged in clusters; color brown to orange or tan. Common on rocks or large red and brown seaweeds on semiprotected rocky shores. Alaska to Santa Barbara. LTZ, IR.

51. Large Ostrich-Plume Hydroid, *Aglaophenia struthionides*. 5–13 cm (2–5") tall, forming yellowish to light red plumes. Common in surf-swept clefts of rocks. San Diego to s. Alaska. LTZ, mainly OR.

52. Fernlike Hydroid, *Abietinaria anguina*. Fernlike sprays often carpet the undersides of rock ledges or shaded boulders. Hydranths of *A. anguina*, like other Leptomedusae, are housed in hard skeletal cups into which their tentacles withdraw at any sign of danger. When left alone, the transparent, flowerlike zooids pop out of their cups to feed. LTZ, IR and OR.

53. Bushy Colonial Hydroid, *Abietinaria greenii*. Similar to above, but covers a wider area and is much more bushy. LTZ, IR.

54. Creeping Hydroids, *Lafoea dumosa* and *L. gracillima*. Irregular creeping colony, sometimes partially erect. Alaska to San Diego, intertidally only in the north. LTZ, IR.

55. Delicate Plume Hydroid, *Plumularia setacea*. Colony up to 2 cm (³⁄₄") tall. It is so glassy it often cannot be seen, but against some backgrounds the tiny, beautiful and delicate sprays of hydranths become visible. Adhesive cells and nematocysts (stinging cells) are used to attack and grab prey. All hydroids use stinging cells to attack or repel enemies. Vancouver Island to s. California. On rocks or seaweeds. LTZ.

56. Large Plume Hydroid, *Plumularia lagenifera*. Larger and more robust than above. Central California to Alaska. LTZ, IR.

55. *Plumularia setacea*
56. *Plumularia lagenifer*
57. *Allopora porphyra*

Order Stylasterina—Hydrocorals

57. Purple Hydrocoral, *Allopora porphyra*. -45- Vivid purple colonies encrust rocky ledges at very low tide levels, often over wide areas. Has star-shaped openings, resembling corals in appearance, though totally different animals. Uncommon, British Columbia to central California. LTZ, IR and less on OR.

Order Chondrophora

58. By-the-Wind Sailor or **Purple Sail Jellyfish**, *Velella velella* -46- Up to 8 cm (3⅛") long; easily recognized by blue color and triangular projecting sail. Floats on offshore waters; sometimes cast ashore in large numbers where they soon die. Worldwide distribution in temperate to tropical waters.

Class Anthozoa
Subclass Zoantharia—Sea anemones and hard corals
Order Corallimorpharia

59. Club-Tipped Anemone, *Corynactis californica.* -38- -47- Column about 1 cm (⅜") in height; diameter 2.5 cm (1") with expanded crown. Commonly red or pink, but also other colors; tentacles are white and club-tipped. Often clusters under overhanging rocks; dislikes sunshine and opens head in the dark. (Not a true anemone but more closely related to the stony corals.) Sonoma Co., California to San Diego. LTZ, IR.

Order Actiniaria

60. Proliferating Anemone, *Epiactis prolifera.* -48- Column 2.5 cm (1") diameter; when expanded up to 5 cm (2"); color highly variable: green, brown, red, etc. with stripes similar in color but darker. Young anemones in brood areas at the base of body; has fluted margin. S. Alaska to s. California. MTZ, LTZ, IR, OR.

61. Red and Green Anemone, *Tealia crassicornis.* -18- Column up to 8–10 cm (3–4") tall, 8 cm (3") in diameter. Red or green, with irregular blotches of green, yellow, or red. Attached to sides and undersurfaces of rocks. Alaska to central California. LTZ, IR.

62. Strawberry Anemone, *Tealia lofotensis.* -49- Column up to 10 cm (4") wide, 15 cm (6") tall. Distinguished by white spots on bright red body. Alaska to San Diego. LTZ, IR.

63. Giant Green Anemone, *Anthopleura xanthogrammica.* -20- Up to 25 cm (10") in diameter, uniformly green. A strong carnivore. Common along whole coast. LTZ, IR and OR.

64. Sandy or **Aggregating Anemone,** *Anthopleura elegantissima.* -19- -50- One of the most abundant anemones. Aggregating individuals up to 8 cm (3") wide across crown; solitary individuals up to 25 cm (10") across crown. Light greenish; commonly covered with bits of gravel or shell to protect against drying up. Found on rock faces, in tidepools or crevices, usually forming squishy colonies that squirt when touched. Alaska to Baja. MTZ, LTZ, IR, some OR.

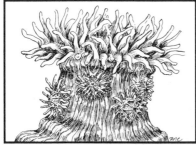

60. *Epiactis prolifera*

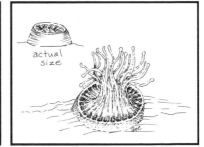

66. *Astrangia lajollaensis*

Order Madreporaria—Stony corals

65. Orange Cup Coral, *Balanophyllia elegans.* -51- Cuplike base up to 1 cm (3/8") in diameter. The lovely orange to yellow polyps (heads) extend their tentacles out of their cuplike skeletons to get food. Puget Sound to s. California. MTZ, LTZ, on rocks where well-sheltered from sunlight. IR.

66. Light Orange Solitary Coral, *Astrangia lajollaensis.* Smaller than above; coral red or orange, with light orange polyps. Usually 36 tentacles, each with a blunt white tip. 7 mm (^{1}/4") high cups. Ridges radiate in a fanlike shape. Southern California. MTZ, IR.

Phylum Platyhelminthes
Class Turbellaria—Freeliving flatworms
Order Polycladida

67. Oval Flatworm, *Alloioplana californica.* Up to 4 cm (1½") long. A thick, firm, oval-shaped body with black, white, and bluish green markings indicating its highly branched digestive tract. Often under rocks on damp sand or gravel. California. HTZ, MTZ.

68. Tapered Flatworm, *Notoplana acticola.* Flat and tapered oval; up to 2.5 cm (1") long, to 6 cm (2⅜") when extended and moving. Tan or pale gray colored with dark markings along the midline. Found under rocks, crawling on wet surfaces. California. HTZ, MTZ, IR.

Order Alloeocoela

69. Phosphorescent Swimming Flatworms, *Monocelis* sp. Tiny little worms seen swimming about in tidepools, or crawling on the surface film of still water, shining like dots of light on dark evenings. The pools are usually rimmed with red algae. MTZ, IR.

Phylum Nemertea—Ribbon worms

70. Twisted Brown Ribbon Worm, *Amphiporus bimaculatus.* -52- From 5–12 cm (2–6") long, but is capable of great expansion, looking like a twisted, flattened brown cord. Two dark spots on the head look like eyes. Body deep red, or brownish red to yellow-

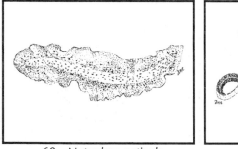

68. *Notoplana acticola*   71. *Emplectonema gracile*

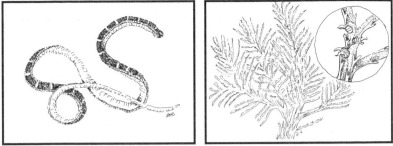

72. Micrura verrilli   *75. Bugula pacifica*

brown. Underside is pale. The proboscis, an easily extended noselike organ, has a central stylet for impaling prey. Alaska to Baja. MTZ, LTZ, IR.

71. Mussel Ribbon Worm, *Emplectonema gracile*. From 5–15 cm (2–6") long usually, but can expand up to 50 cm (20"). Dark green to yellowish green above, pale below; often looking like tangled pieces of rubber bands. Common in mussel beds. Does not break up easily when disturbed like other nemerteans. Alaska to Baja. HTZ, MTZ, IR.

72. Lavender and White Ribbon Worm, *Micrura verrilli*. Up to 46 cm (18") long; dorsal surface covered with rectangular blocks of lavender or reddish purple; lower surface pure white. Under rocks and in beds of algae or eelgrass. Alaska to Monterey Bay. LTZ, IR.

73. Light-Ringed Ribbon Worm, *Lineus vegetus*. Up to 15 cm (6") long. Body is brown with numerous encircling lighter rings; often coils in a tight spiral. Under rocks. Pacific Grove to La Jolla. LTZ, IR.

74. Pink String Ribbon Worm, *Procephalothrix major*. Pinkish and stringy; only 3 mm ($^1/_{16}$") wide, but may reach over 1 m (40") long! Under stones on hard sand or clay. Big Sur to Ensenada, Mexico. LTZ, IR and OR.

Phylum Bryozoa—Moss animals

Bryozoa often look like fur or like hydroids in frondlike colonies. But when examined closely with a magnifying glass, it is seen that bryozoans snap back into their compartments, whereas hydroids withdraw slowly.

75. Pacific Branching or **Bird Beak Bryozoan**, *Bugula pacifica*. About 2–7 cm ($^3/_4$–$2^3/_4$") tall. Purple or yellowish and even lighter; branches in a mildly spiral fashion. Largest specimens are found in the northern part of the range. Alaska to s. California. LTZ, IR.

76. Delicate White Bryozoan, *Tricellaria occidentalis*. Appears in delicate, white branching sprays, not over 2 cm ($^3/_4$") high, hanging down in rocky crevices, or at the bases of surfgrass. British Columbia to Baja. LTZ, IR.

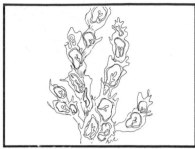

76. *Tricellaria occidentalis*

77. *Phidolopora pacifica*

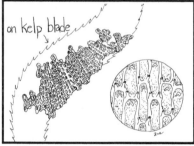

78. *Membranipora membranacea*

80. *Barentsia ramosa*

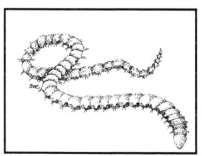

82. *Arabella iricolor*

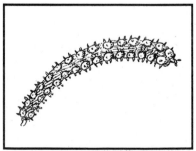

83. *Halosydna brevisetosa*

77. Lacy Orange Bryozoan, *Phidolopora pacifica.* Up to 6.5 cm (2½") high. Colonies form lacy calcareous, orange clusters on rocks in deep sheltered tidepools; latticelike in appearance. British Columbia to Mexico. LTZ, IR.

78. White-Encrusting Bryozoan, *Membranipora membranacea.* Forms small irregular (sometimes round) white encrustations mostly on the LTZ kelps, occasionally on shells or wood; colony has fine honeycomb appearance; individual cells (zooids) rectangular, covered by a lightly calcified membrane, and with a calcified rim. Under a magnifying glass intricate and beautiful patterns can be seen radiating in irregular rows from the center. Most of coast. LTZ, IR.

79. Rose-Colored Bryozoan, *Eurystomella bilabiata.* Color rose-red, red-orange, or brown; usually forms beautiful, flat encrustations on rocks and old shells, the delicate traceries visible best with a magnifying glass. From Alaska to Mexico. LTZ, IR.

Phylum Entoprocta

80. Flower-Headed Entoproct, *Barentsia ramosa.* An individual of the colony consists of a slender stalk, from 1–2 cm (³⁄₈–³⁄₄") long, topped by a tentacled, flowerlike head. Unlike hydroids and bryozoa, these creatures contract their tentacles inward when disturbed. The flowerlike heads form thick-matted colonies in caves and on rocky underhangs. Central California. LTZ, IR.

Phylum Annelida—Segmented worms
Class Polychaeta—Segmented marine worms

Segmented marine worms are characterized by having many bristlelike appendages (which is the meaning of polychaete) projecting from either side.

81. Leaf-Legged Paddle Worm, *Anaitides medipapillata.* Up to 17 cm (6½") long. Body is purple-blue with brown or creamish trimmings and iridescent glints. Its appendages are broad and leaf-shaped, hence the common name of "paddle worm." Found in holdfasts of large seaweeds and under rocks. Central California to Mexico. LTZ, IR.

82. Green Iridescent Worm, *Arabella iricolor.* Length usually 15–20 cm (6–8"), can be up to 60 cm (2'). Highly iridescent, green, very slim and breakable. In holdfasts on rocks or burrowing in sand. Canada to Mexico. LTZ, IR.

83. Common Scale Worm, *Halosydna brevisetosa.* Up to 11 cm (4¼") long when living commensally; 18 pairs of oval dorsal scales. Free-living sheltered in mussel beds or plant holdfasts; commensal in tubes of larger marine worms. Alaska to Baja. LTZ, IR.

84. Dark-Spotted Scale Worm, *Arctonoe pulchra.* Distinguished by a dark spot on each scale. Up to 7 cm (2¾") long. Found as a commensal on California sea cucumbers, the giant chiton, and several other intertidal invertebrates. Alaska to Baja. LTZ, IR.

87. Cirriformia luxuriosa   *90. Eudistylia polymorpha*

85. Yellow Scale Worm, *Arctonoe vittata.* Up to 8–10 cm (3–4") long, pale to light yellow. Lives commensally in the gills of chitons, snails, and seastars. Has 30 or more pairs of smooth, oval scales on back. Alaska to Ecuador. MTZ, LTZ, IR.

86. Two-Tentacled Spionid Worm, *Boccardia proboscidea.* These colonial worms dig into shale rocks or clay, making U-shaped burrows and protruding two tiny tentacles from one end of them. In sandy tidepools. British Columbia to s. California. LTZ, IR.

87. Hairy-Gilled Spionid Worm, *Cirriformia luxuriosa.* Up to 15 cm (6") long, white, tapering gradually from head to tail; reddish gills and orange-red feeding tentacles wave from the upper half of the body. Burrows in mud under rocks and among the roots of surfgrass; its gills are often visible on the surface. In black, even foul, mud. Central California to Baja. HTZ to LTZ, IR.

88. Prolific Chaetopterid Worm, *Phyllochaetopterus prolifica.* Inhabits clusters of very thin, membranous tubes 1–1.5 mm ($^{1}\!/_{16}$") diameter, 10–15 cm (4–6") long, matting large areas of vertical or slightly overhanging rocks or pilings, especially where they meet a sandy substratum. British Columbia to s. California. LTZ, IR.

89. Black Cirratulid Worm, *Dodecaceria fewkesi.* Up to 4 cm (1½") long. Dense colonies of these dark brown to black, tube-building worms mass on rocks, usually limestone, and sometimes on the shells of the red abalone. British Columbia to s. California. MTZ to LTZ, IR.

90. Feather-Duster Worm, *Eudistylia polymorpha.* -53- Up to 25 cm (10") long. Inhabits a tough, parchmentlike tube reaching far down into the crevices of rocks, as far as 46 cm (18"). Beautiful gills, maroon, orange, or brown colored, protrude out of the tube into the waters of the tidepool, looking like a colorful feather duster; but they snap back quickly into their tube if disturbed. Alaska to s. California. LTZ, IR.

91. Fan-Headed Worm, *Sabella crassicornis.* Similar to *E. polymorpha,* but only about 5 cm (2") long. Distal end bears a beautiful maroon, fan-shaped cluster of gills dotted with paired eyespots. Makes a membranous, sand-encrusted tube around its body; in crevices or under substratum in tidepools. Alaska to s. California. LTZ, IR.

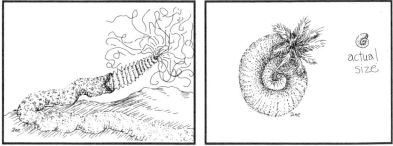

92. *Thelepus crispus*   95. *Spirorbis sp.*

92. Hairy-Headed Terebellid Worm, *Thelepus crispus.* Commonly up to 15 cm (6") long, sometimes up to 28 cm (11"). A sedentary worm that digs a hole between or under rocks and inhabits a case made of tiny pebbles and other debris cemented together. Body brown or flesh-colored; reddish gill filaments extend profusely from the head region. Burrowing habitat. Alaska to s. California. MTZ, LTZ, IR.

93. Amber-Topped Honeycomb Worm, *Sabellaria cementarium.* Up to 8 cm (3") long. Worms build tubes of cemented sand grains, sometimes solitary, usually joined together into honeycomblike structures that can form large reefs. The operculum, or lidlike structure that stoppers up the tube when the worm is retracted, is amber colored. When submerged by the tide, the worm's ciliated lavender tentacles stretch out of the tube to draw food into its mouth. Alaska to San Diego. LTZ, IR.

94. Black-Topped Honeycomb Worm, *Phragmatopoma californica.* Up to 5 cm (2") long. Forms similar honeycomb-like tube structures as above; rarely solitary. Operculum is black; anterior end bears crown of lavender tentacles. Central California to Baja. MTZ, LTZ, IR.

95. Small Spirorbid Worms, *Spirorbis* sp. Tiny white calcareous tubes (1 mm wide) of these worms are tightly coiled; their almost microscopic, red to orange tentacles, visible at the ends of the tubes, catch microscopic animals. Found on various substrata, such as rocks, seaweed, and piers. MTZ, LTZ.

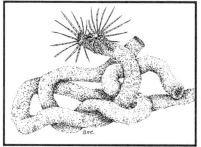

96. *Serpula vermicularis*

96. White-Tubed Worm, *Serpula vermicularis.* -23- Occupies white calcareous tubes up to 10 cm (4") long, often coiled, and cylindrical; operculum red. Red, pink, or orange hairlike gills snap back into tubes if touched. Currents bring in small creatures they catch. Alaska to San Diego. On undersurfaces and sides of rocks. LTZ, IR.

97. Mussel Worm, *Nereis vexillosa.* -24- From 5–30 cm (2–12") long. Often iridescent green-brown in color. Segments with up to 118 leglike projections. Its wicked-looking jaws can bite, so be careful. Often in mussel beds; sought for bait by fishermen. Abundant Alaska to Baja. HTZ, MTZ, IR and OR.

98. Giant Mussel Worm, *Neanthes brandti.* Up to 1 meter (3′) long; broad body with many projections on the proboscis. These giant worms are seen most often in spring and early summer when they swarm on the water's surface to spawn; they are attracted to a light at night. Alaska to San Pedro. HTZ to LTZ, IR, OR.

Phylum Sipuncula—Peanut worms

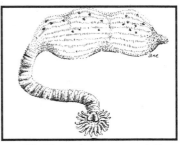

99. Dotted Peanut Worm, *Phascolosoma agassizii.* Up to 12 cm (4¾") long. A 5 cm (2") specimen (closer to average) can extend its trunk with a bush of short stubby tentacles at the end to 15 cm (6"). Skin rough textured, light brown, frequently with brown to purplish spots. Abundant under rocks, in muddy crevices, in sand, and among the roots of surfgrass and holdfasts. Alaska to Baja. MTZ, LTZ, IR.

99. Phascolosoma agassizii

100. Flowering Peanut Worm, *Themiste pyroides.* Rich brown-colored worm with a bush of flowerlike tentacles at the head. Average length 10–12 cm (4–4¾") but reaching 20 cm (8"). Put in a bowl of seawater and left undisturbed under subdued light, it will flower beautifully. Common under rocks and in holes and crevices. British Columbia to Baja. LTZ, IR.

Phylum Arthropoda—Segmented invertebrates with jointed limbs
Class Pycnogonida—Sea spiders

101. Giant Sea Spider, *Ammothea hilgendorfi.* Body up to 2.5 cm (1") long, amber colored with darker bands on its long, gangling legs. Often found camouflaged among hydroids, where it slowly climbs about. Genus has many smaller forms. Alaska to Baja. LTZ, IR.

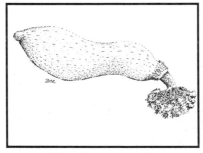

100. Themiste pyroides

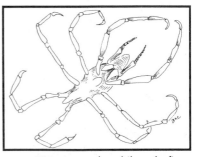

101. Ammothea hilgendorfi

Class Crustacea—Crabs, shrimps, barnacles, and their relatives

Subclass Copepoda

102. Splash Pool Copepod, *Tigriopus californicus.* About 1–2 mm (1⁄16") long. Fast-moving, very tiny, red buglike crustaceans in warm, brackish splash pools near or above the high-tide line. Has conspicuous hooked antennae. Alaska to Baja. SPLZ, IR.

Subclass Cirripedia—Barnacles

103. Acorn Barnacle, *Balanus glandula.* Shell 2 cm (3⁄4") or less wide. Dingy white to gray; the sharp projecting shells often crowd together on rock faces, looking like the cells of a honeycomb. Brightly-colored appendages come out at high tide to sweep food into their mouths. Alaska to Baja. SPLZ to MTZ, IR, OR, and rocky shores of bays and estuaries.

102. *Tigriopus californicus*

103. *Balanus glandula*
104. *Semibalanus cariosus*

104. Thatched Barnacle, *Semibalanus cariosus.* This strongly-ridged, conical barnacle, often with a thatched-roof appearance, may be up to 5 cm (2") in basal diameter; but in crowded conditions up to 10 cm (4") in height and 2 mm (1⁄16") in diameter. Young have less eroded ridges in symmetrical, starlike pattern; gray to white. Alaska to Morro Bay, California. MTZ, LTZ, IR, OR, and rocky shores of bays and estuaries.

105. Small Northern Barnacle, *Chthamalus dalli.* Shell up to 8 mm (1⁄4") basal diameter and half as high, usually pale gray, and with a consistently clean-cut shape. Never crowds as closely together as *Semibalanus.* Found mainly on the rocks of bays, estuaries, and sounds from Alaska to San Diego; fewer south of Monterey. SPLZ, HTZ, IR.

106. Small Southern Barnacle, *Chthamalus fissus.* Almost identical in appearance to the

105–106. *Chthamalus sp.*

above species; gray to brown. With *C. dalli* the muscle attachment scar has strong ridges; with *C. fissus* there is a smooth depression. San Francisco to Baja. SPLZ, HTZ, IR. Common in bays and estuaries.

107. Goose-Neck Barnacle, *Pollicipes polymerus*. -54- Up to 8 cm (3") tall. Shells, chalky white plates when dry, surmounting a black and wrinkled neck, form groups of clusters pointing in the same direction. One form of this species having brilliant rainbow colors is restricted to caves or rocks protected from direct sunlight. Alaska to Baja. On wave-swept rocks, HTZ, MTZ, OR.

108. Red Thatched Barnacle, *Tetraclita rubescens*. Diameter usually up to 3 cm (1⅛"). In adults brick-red color and thatched-hut appearance are distinctive. Young, uneroded shells are white. San Francisco to Baja. MTZ, LTZ, OR.

Subclass Malacostraca—Shrimps, crabs, rock lice, etc.
Order Mysidacea—Opossum shrimps

109. Southern Opossum Shrimp, *Acanthomysis costata*. Up to 1.3 cm (½") long. Called opossum shrimps because the female carries her eggs in a pouch on her lower legs. Swarms of these tiny, delicate and transparent shrimps appear in the tidepools in various years. They have huge eyes and long, delicate legs. Southern California. MTZ, IR.

110. Northern Opossum Shrimp, *Acanthomysis sculpta*. Very similar to above, but mainly found from central California to Washington. MTZ, IR.

Order Isopoda—Pill bugs

111. Dark-Backed Isopod, *Cirolana harfordi*. Looks like the common land pill bug; pale gray to black; up to 2 cm (¾") long. British Columbia to Mexico. Very common under rocks at all tide levels.

112. Sea Urchin Isopod, *Colidotea rostrata*. Another pill bug, only found hidden in the spines of sea urchins. Up to 12 mm (⅜") long; matches color of host. Southern California. LTZ, IR.

108. *Tetraclita rubescens*   111. *Cirolana harfori*

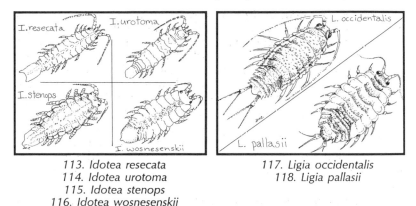

113. Idotea resecata
114. Idotea urotoma
115. Idotea stenops
116. Idotea wosnesenskii

117. Ligia occidentalis
118. Ligia pallasii

113. Cut-Tailed Isopod, *Idotea resecata.* Up to 4 cm (1½") long. Usually yellow-brown in color to match the kelp it eats; green on eelgrass; tailpiece ends with a concave border. Alaska to Baja. Rocky shores of bays and estuaries. MTZ.

114. Paddle-Tailed Isopod, *Idotea urotoma.* Body up to 1.6 cm (⅝") long with the paddlelike tail, characteristic of *Idotea* sp. Color variable but often brown. Puget Sound to Baja. Under rocks. MTZ, LTZ.

115. Large Paddle-Tailed Isopod, *Idotea stenops.* Up to 4 cm (1½") long, and stout; one of the largest of the isopods. Body olive green to brown. Often found on the brown feather boa kelp, *Egregia,* and under boulders and rocks. Alaska to Baja. MTZ, LTZ, OR.

116. Round-Tailed Isopod, *Idotea wosnesenskii.* Up to 3.5 cm (1⅜"); usually very dark; tailpiece rounded with a small tooth at the tip. Common in mussel beds, on seaweeds, and under rocks. Alaska to s. California. MTZ, LTZ, IR and OR.

117. Western Sea Roach, *Ligia occidentalis.* -55- Up to 2.5 cm (1") long; its shape, speed, and habits similar to a cockroach; brownish gray, mottled; two long, forked spines project from the end of the body. These fast moving scavengers above the intertidal zone are dark colored in the daylight, turning paler at night. Often under rocks and in crevices. Sonoma Co., California, to Mexico. SPLZ, OR.

118. Northern Sea Roach, *Ligia pallasii.* Up to 3.5 cm (1 ⅜") long; has much shorter forked tail spines than *L. occidentalis,* and broader body. Often with green algae. Santa Cruz to Alaska. SPLZ, OR.

Order Amphipoda—Beach hoppers, sand fleas, and skeleton shrimp

Amphipods are found often in rockweeds, which you can shake over a dishpan to disclose. The number of species with similar characteristics is exceedingly numerous, so specific identification should be left to the specialist.

119. Saddle-marked Beach Hopper, *Ampithoe humeralis.* Saddle-shaped markings on white of back. One of the common species of Ampithoidae, tiny beach hoppers or sand fleas, usually 1 cm (³⁄₈") or less long, found in and under rockweed of the same color. The antennae are more than half the length of the body, and one is thicker than the other. These beach hoppers jump about very briskly. Found from Puget Sound southward. HTZ, MTZ, IR.

120. Common Sand Flea, *Atylopsis* sp. Also tiny and color-adapted to rockweed like *Ampithoe.* Both of these genera have clawlike endings on the legs to cling to the rockweed and, typical of beach hoppers, are compressed laterally (up and down), enabling them to hop with ease. Exceedingly common; most of coast. HTZ, MTZ.

121. Mussel Bed Sand Flea, *Elasmopus rapax.* This is another common beach hopper, or sand flea, but smaller (5 mm or less), found in great numbers in MTZ mussel beds. Most of coast.

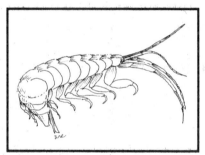
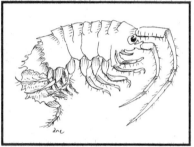

119. *Ampithoe sp.*   122. *Melita sp.*

122. Common Tidepool Sand Flea, *Melita* sp. Small sand fleas, very common under rocks in HTZ to MTZ. Most of coast.

123. Slaty Green Beach Hopper, *Traskorchestia* sp. Often found feeding on decaying seaweed; lustrous slaty green; one antenna is shorter than the other; second thoracic leg has pincerlike end. All coasts. SPLZ to MTZ, IR.

124. Splash-Zone Beach Hopper, *Traskorchestia traskiana.* 1 cm (³⁄₈") or less long; dull green or gray-brown with bluish legs. It actively jumps about above the high tide level, but hides in cast-up seaweeds when the tide goes out. Very short second antennae. Most of coast. SPLZ.

125. Tunicate Amphipod, *Polycheria osborni.* About 3–8 mm (¹⁄₈–¹⁄₄") long. The semi-transparent animals burrow in the sheetlike gelatinous mass of

125. *Polycheria osborni*

the tunicate, *Aplidium californicum*, then lie on their backs in the cavities, waving legs and tentacles to catch microscopic foods. Even when swimming they move with back down. Oregon to s. California. I TZ, IR.

126. Common Skeleton Shrimp, *Caprella californica*. Up to 3.5 cm (1³⁄₈") long. Its thin, sticklike body has large, hooked claws by which it clings to kelp fronds or to eelgrass, often seeming like part of them; they often bow slowly, resembling a marine version of the praying mantis. Commonly brown, but also red or green depending on the background. Common in eelgrass flats. Central and southern California. LTZ, IR.

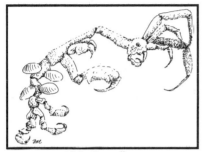

| 126. Caprella sp. | 128. Betaeus longidactylus |

127. Pink-Banded Skeleton Shrimp, *Metacaprella kennerlyi*. About 2.5 cm (1") long. Like other skeleton shrimps it may be seen swaying or solemnly bowing as it clings, well-camouflaged, to colonies of hydroids, commonly on *Abietinaria*. Body pink-banded. Alaska to s. California. LTZ.

Order Decapoda—Shrimps, lobsters, and crabs
Infraorder Caridea—Shrimps

128. Long-Fingered Shrimp, *Betaeus longidactylus*. 4 cm (1½") long with very long pincers in males. Body and claws are olive brown to blue or blue-green, with red legs, and a fringe of yellow hairs on the end of the abdomen. Under rocks and in pools. Monterey Bay to Gulf of California. MTZ, IR.

129. Noisy Pistol Shrimp, *Alpheus clamator*. Less than 4 cm (1½") long, with a long snapping pincer on the right foreleg. Makes metallic clicking noises or an explosive snap if disturbed. Very active and hard to catch; body tan with some dark brown markings. Tidepools and crevices on rocky shores. San Francisco to Baja. LTZ, IR.

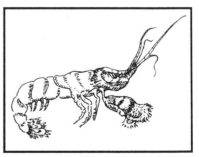

129. *Alpheus clamator*

130. California Pistol Shrimp, *Alpheus californiensis*. Almost identifical with *A. clamator* but with a smaller snapping claw. Found in or about the roots of eelgrass; mud flats in bays. San Pedro to Baja.

131. Red Rock Shrimp, *Lysmata californica*. Up to 7 cm (2¾") long. Cream-colored with broken red stripes running from front to back; appendages are red. Called a "cleaning" shrimp because it picks parasites and other materials from the bodies of other tidepool animals; often clustered in large groups. Common among rocks and seaweed. Santa Barbara and south. LTZ, IR.

132. Slender Green Shrimp, *Hippolyte californiensis*. About 4 cm (1½") long or less; green, delicate, very slender. Carapace has a pronounced forward projection, with 3 to 5 teeth on both lower and upper margins. In the daytime it darts under rocks and in crevices; at night it swims freely among the eelgrass of bay and estuary habitat. Bodega Bay to Baja. LTZ.

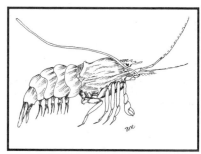

| *131. Lysmata californica* | *134. Heptacarpus pictus* |

133. Broken-Back Shrimps, *Heptacarpus* sp. From about 2–4 cm (¾–1½") long. Called "broken back" because they characteristically bend their tails rapidly under and forward to swim backwards. Those found in higher tidepools are smaller and transparent; those in the lower tide zone are opaque and larger; the variety of coloring of these shrimps camouflages them well. Under rocks in pools. Most of coast. LTZ, IR.

134. Red-Banded Transparent Shrimp, *Heptacarpus pictus*. Up to about 2.4 cm (1") long. Lovely transparent and greenish shrimp, often with oblique red bands. Darts backward, as do most of these shrimps, by flexing its tail. Abundant in tidepools from San Francisco to San Diego. MTZ, IR.

135. Eelgrass Transparent Shrimp, *Heptacarpus paludicola*. Almost indistinguishable from *H. pictus*, except that it is much more common in eelgrass beds and on mud flats. Rostrum is nearly as long as the rest of the body armor. Humboldt Co., California, to Bodega Bay.

Infraorder Thalassinidea—Ghost and mud shrimps

136. Bay Ghost Shrimp, *Callianassa californiensis*. -56- Up to 11.5 cm (4½") long; body whitish and crayfishlike. Carapace smooth with unequal-sized pincers. Abundant burrowing in sand and mud flats of bays and estuaries. S. Alaska to Baja. MTZ.

Infraorder Anomura—Hermit, porcelain, and mole crabs

137. Flat Porcelain Crab, *Petrolisthes cinctipes.* Up to 2.4 cm (1") long. This small, flat, reddish brown crab is the most abundant under-rock inhabitant of the high and middle tide zones. Their flat bodies allow them to dash under rocks or to hide in crevices or mussel beds. If pinned by a rock their autotomizing ability allows them to break free and regenerate a new limb quickly. British Columbia to Pt. Conception, California. HTZ, MTZ, IR and OR.

138. Thick-Clawed Porcelain Crab, *Pachycheles rudis.* -36- Only slightly smaller than *P. cinctipes,* but recognized by the thicker, heavily granulated, unequal pincers; dull brown color. Common under rocks, in kelp holdfasts, beneath eelgrass root mats, on wharf pilings. Alaska to Baja. MTZ, LTZ, IR.

139. Umbrella-Backed Crab, *Cryptolithodes sitchensis.* -57- Carapace up to 7 cm (2¾") wide, 5 cm (2") long. Large umbrella-like carapace covers back and hides the legs; color extremely variable. Under rocks. Alaska to San Diego. LTZ, IR.

140. Fuzzy Crab, *Hapalogaster cavicauda.* Carapace to about 2 cm (¾") long. This very fuzzy crab is covered with short brownish hair; often has an enlarged abdomen. Usually under rocks where, if uncovered, it generally remains motionless, looking like part of the rock. Mendocino Co., California, to Baja. LTZ, IR.

141. Red-Brown Bristly Crab, *Hapalogaster mertensii.* Similar to *H. cavicauda* except that it is covered by bristly brownish or reddish brown tufts instead of fine hair. Alaska to Puget Sound. LTZ, IR.

 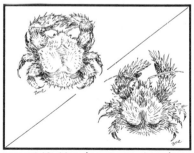

138. Pachycheles rudis   *140. Hapalogaster cavicauda*
                           141. Hapalogaster mertensii

142. Hole-Loving Crab, *Oedignathus inermis.* Carapace up to 3 cm (1¼") long, dull brown with scalelike plates; large abdomen and one of its claws is especially large. Moves slowly, and lives mainly in holes, abandoned sea-urchin pits, and rock crevices. Alaska to Monterey Bay. LTZ, IR.

145. *Pagurus samuelis*   148. *Cancer productus*
149. *Cancer oregonensis*

143. Hairy-Legged Hermit Crab, *Pagurus hirsutiusculus.* Up to 7 cm (2¾") overall length in quiet northern waters; much smaller and less hairy in California. Body usually brown; legs hairy banded with white or bluish white. Finds homes in the shells of large rock snails. Rocky shores of bays and estuaries. Alaska to San Diego. MTZ, LTZ, IR.

144. Giant Hermit Crab, *Pagurus beringanus.* Up to 10 or 12 cm (4-5") in size. Thicker than *P. hirsutiusculus* and with short, bright red spines on claws; usual color brown marked with light green and scarlet. Often found in Oregon triton shells. Bays and estuaries of Oregon and Washington. LTZ, IR.

145. High Tide Zone Hermit Crab, *Pagurus samuelis.* -32- Carapace up to 2 cm (¾") long. Small size, scarlet antennae, and bright blue bands at tips of feet distinguish this hermit crab. Prefers the shell of the black turban snail, over which it will fight another hermit for possession. British Columbia to Baja. HTZ, MTZ, IR.

146. Middle Tide Zone Hermit Crab, *Pagurus hemphilli.* Carapace up to 2 cm (¾") long; brownish red dotted with blue granules. Distinguished by wrist of big claw bent at a sharp angle. Alaska to Channel Islands. MTZ, LTZ, IR.

Infraorder Brachyura—The true crabs

147. Red-Spotted Cancer Crab, *Cancer attennarius.* (Also called Pacific Rock Crab.) -33- Carapace up to 13 cm (5") wide; reddish brown, but most easily identified by red spots on its light undersurface. Snaps claws and makes bubbles when disturbed. Under rocks and in pools. Coos Bay, Oregon, to Baja. LTZ, IR.

148. Red Cancer Crab, *Cancer productus.* Carapace up to 16 cm (6½") wide. Distinctive brick-red color. The young are white or striped in a variety of colors. Often partly buried in sandy areas under rocks. At night it is the dominant, stalking tyrant of the LTZ pools. Common in bays and estuaries. Alaska to San Diego. LTZ, IR.

149. Oregon Cancer Crab, *Cancer oregonensis.* Carapace up to about 3 cm (1¼") in males, 4.5 cm (1¾") in females. Distinctive round carapace, dark red with lighter undersurface; hairy legs have dark claws. Alaska to s. California, but rare south of Pt. Arena.

Commonly lives among beds of mussels and barnacles, on which it feeds. LTZ, IR.

150. Lined Shore Crab, *Pachygrapsus crassipes*. -30- Carapace up to 4.5 cm (1¾") wide. Usually green in color with wavy white lines or stripes, but can be dark red or another color variation and with or without stripes; squat, flat, squarish body. Sometimes pugnacious and assertive, either offering to fight an intruder or scurrying away sideways and backwards in alarm. Central Oregon to Baja. HTZ, MTZ, IR.

151. Purple Shore Crab, *Hemigrapsus nudus*. -31- Carapace up to 5.5 cm (2¼") wide in males, 3.5 cm (1⅜") in females; color usually purple, sometimes greenish yellow or reddish brown. Purple or red spots on the claws are distinctive. Pugnacious scavenger in rockweeds. Alaska to Baja. MTZ, LTZ, IR.

152. Lumpy Red Crab, *Paraxanthias taylori*. Carapace to around 4 cm (1½") wide in females, 2.5 cm (1") in males. Dark or dull red color with numerous large lumps, particularly on claws. Under rocks and in crevices. Monterey to Baja, but more common in the south. MTZ, LTZ, IR.

152. Paraxanthias taylori

153. Scyra acutifrons

153. Sharp-Nosed Masking Crab, *Scyra acutifrons*. Width up to 3.7 cm (1½"). Narrow, two-horned beak protrudes forward from pear-shaped body. Often camouflages itself with sponges, bryozoans, barnacles, and other such sea creatures that surround it. Like most masking crabs, it moves slowly and is difficult to see. Among algae and on or under rocks. Alaska to Baja, but rare in s. California. LTZ, IR.

154. Sponge-Covered Kelp Crab, *Mimulus foliatus*. Carapace up to 4 cm (1½") wide; red, yellow, or red-brown; shield-shaped; often covered with growths of sponges, which add to its coloration. Legs with light crossbands. Common on kelp holdfasts, mostly subtidal. Alaska to San Diego. LTZ, IR.

154. Mimulus foliatus

157. Taliepus nuttallii

158. Loxorhynchus crispatus

159–161. Lophopanopeus sp.

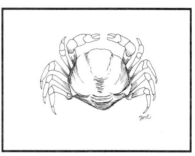

162. Fabia subquadrata

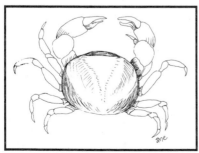

163. Pinnixa tubicola

164. Pilumnus spinohirsutus

155. Shield-Backed Kelp Crab, *Pugettia producta.* -34- -35- Carapace up to 9 cm (3½") wide, smooth and shield-shaped; reddish or olive brown color. Slim but powerful and dangerous claws; sharp spines on carapace and legs. It uses its spines to cling to seaweed on which it feeds. Common on rocks or in kelp. Alaska to Baja. LTZ, IR.

156. Graceful Kelp Crab, *Pugettia gracilis.* Up to 4 cm (1½") wide. More graceful looking than above, but with the same powerful claws and dangerous spines. Carapace brown, yellow, or red. Alaska to s. California. In eelgrass and kelp on rocky shores. LTZ, IR.

157. Southern Kelp Crab, *Taliepus nuttallii.* Carapace up to 9 cm (3½") wide (half that in females). Purple or red-brown with blotches of lighter coloring. Like other kelp crabs, it is dangerous to handle because of the sharp spines. Has a preference for brown algae. Santa Barbara, California, to Baja. LTZ, IR.

158. Large Masking Crab, *Loxorhynchus crispatus.* Carapace width up to 9 cm (3½") in males. Grotesquely shaped with lumpy body usually covered with growing seaweeds and other attached sea creatures; very sluggish and hard to see. N. California to Baja. LTZ (although more common subtidally), IR.

159. Southern Black-Clawed Crab, *Lophopanopeus frontalis.* Carapace up to 2.4 cm (1") wide (females about half this). A dark band on the thumb of the pincer extends far backward and up. Under rocks in bays and among clusters of mussels on pilings. Santa Monica Bay to Baja. LTZ, IR.

160. Central Black-Clawed Crab, *Lophopanopeus leucomanus leucomanus.* Males are slightly smaller than *L. frontalis* but the females are larger. Upper and outer surface of claw irregularly pitted; separated by a network of ridges. Dark brown or black band crosses finger of claw. Under rocks. Monterey to Baja. LTZ, IR.

161. Northern Black-Clawed Crab, *Lophopanopeus bellus bellus.* Carapace width up to 3.4 cm (1⅜"). Variously colored, but it has a distinctive black band across finger and thumb of claw. Commonly burrows in sand under rocks in bays and estuaries. Alaska to Monterey, but rare in southern part of range. LTZ, IR.

162. Parasitic Pea Crab or **Mussel Crab,** *Fabia subquadrata.* Carapace up to 16 mm (⅝") wide (males half the size). Top surface is shaped like a pumpkin, with two longitudinal grooves extending halfway back on the carapace. Body whitish, marked with orange spots. Both sexes commensal and parasitic on mussels and mollusks. Alaska to San Diego. LTZ, OR.

163. Polychaete Worm Pea Crab, *Pinnixa tubicola.* Tiny pea crab (about 1 cm) living commensally in the tubes of polychaete worms. Alaska to San Diego. MTZ, LTZ, IR.

164. Hairy Under-Rock Crab, *Pilumnus spinohirsutus.* To about 3.5 cm (1⅜") wide. A retiring, extremely hairy and spiny crab. Light brown color. Among and under rocks, often hidden in sand. Los Angeles Co., California, to Baja. LTZ, IR.

Phylum Mollusca—Shellfish
Class Polyplacophora—Chitons, or sea cradles

165. Lined Chiton, *Tonicella lineata*. -58- Up to 5 cm (2") long; elongate-oval; found on rocks covered with coralline algae. Usually light reddish, marked with zigzag lines of alternating colors; girdle yellowish or greenish, often alternately banded. Alaska to southern California. MTZ, LTZ, IR.

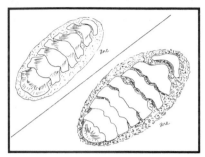
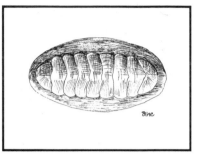

166. Stenoplax heathiana	*168. Ischnochiton regularis*
167. Stenoplax conspicua	

166. Green Marbled Chiton, *Stenoplax heathiana*. Up to 11 cm (4⅜") long and twice as long as wide. Pale grayish or brownish cream, often spotted with light to dark greenish gray. Common under rocks embedded in sand. Fort Bragg to Baja. MTZ, LTZ, IR.

167. Conspicuous Chiton, *Stenoplax conspicua*. Up to 10 cm (4") long (half as wide). Green, brownish, or mottled. Girdle is wide and thick, densely covered with short, velvety bristles. Found under smooth rocks in sand. Santa Barbara to Baja. LTZ, IR.

168. Slaty Blue Chiton, *Ischnochiton regularis*. Up to 5 cm (2") long; intermediate lateral areas with delicate radiating threads. Uniform slaty blue or slaty gray color; oblong. Found under smooth rocks in sand. Mendocino Co., California, to Monterey. LTZ, IR.

169. Ribbed Chiton, *Callistochiton crassicostatus*. Up to 5 cm (2") long; oblong. Mottled grayish green to light brown with high keels on the plates. Girdle narrow, cream-colored with white bands. Under rocks. Monterey Bay to Baja. MTZ, LTZ, IR.

170. Mossy Chiton, *Mopalia muscosa*. -15- Up to 9 cm (3½") long; oval. Stiff, brownish red bristles on the girdle are distinctive. Plates are generally dull brown, blackish olive or grayish. Common on rocks and in tidepools. British Columbia to Baja. MTZ, LTZ, IR.

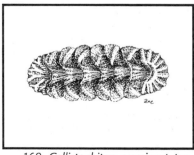

169. Callistochiton crassicostatus

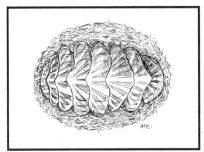

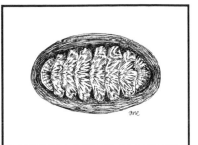

171. Mopalia ciliata　　　　　*172. Mopalia lignosa*

171. Hairy Chiton, *Mopalia ciliata*. Up to 7.5 cm (3") long. Oval-shaped and variously colored, often with patches of green, red, brown, or yellow in combination; distinctive notch at tail end; girdle wide and thick, densely covered with curly brown hairs. In crevices and under rocks. Alaska to Baja. MTZ, LTZ, IR and OR.

172. Woody Chiton, *Mopalia lignosa*. Up to 7 cm (2³⁄₄") long; oval. Distinct beak on the posterior plate; grayish, bluish, or greenish, streaked with brown, purple-brown, or white. Not very hairy; girdle narrow and orange on underside. On sides of or under large rocks. Alaska to Pt. Conception. MTZ, LTZ, IR and OR.

173. California Chiton, *Nuttallina californica*. Up to 5 cm (2") long; elongate to oval. Girdle wide, brownish, with short, rigid spines. Plates dark brown to blackish, sometimes with stripes or blotches of white. Common clinging to rocks exposed to strong surf. Puget Sound to San Diego. HTZ, MTZ, OR.

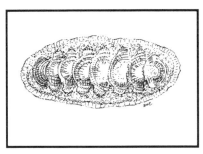

173. Nuttallina californica

174. Black Chiton, *Katharina tunicata*. -17- Up to 12 cm (4³⁄₄") long. Thick, leathery black girdle partly covers the shell plates. One of the few chitons that does not retreat from direct sunlight. Alaska to s. California, but more abundant northward. MTZ, LTZ, OR and IR (where there are strong currents).

175. Giant or **Gumboot Chiton**, *Cryptochiton stelleri* -16- -37- Up to 33 cm (13") long. Brick-red or reddish brown; thick, leathery mantle covers all shell plates. Sometimes mistaken for a giant sea cucumber. Usually next to deep pools or channels, Alaska to southern California. LTZ, IR.

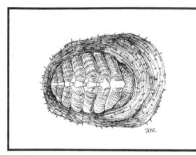

176. Placiphorella velata

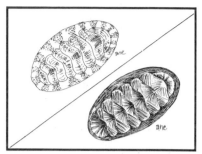

177. Lepidozona mertensii
178. Lepidozona cooperi

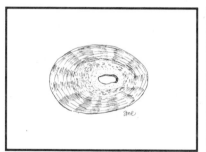

180. Fissurella volcano

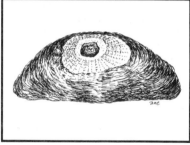

181. Megathura crenulata

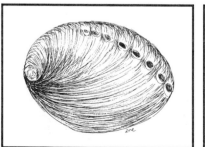

182. Haliotis cracherodii

184. Haliotis fulgens

176. Veiled Chiton, *Placiphorella velata.* Up to 5 cm (2") long. Round-oval in shape; brownish or reddish, mottled or streaked with white, green, beige, or black. An active predator, using its expanded girdle flap to trap victims. In crevices or under rocks. Alaska to Baja. ITZ, IR.

177. Mottled Red Chiton, *Lepidozona mertensii.* Up to 5 cm (2") long. Straight sides and angular ridges. Overall red color, sometimes with white blotches; girdle reddish with lighter bands. Alaska to Mexico. LTZ, IR.

178. Dull Brown Chiton, *Lepidozona cooperi.* Similar to *L. mertensii,* but dull brown. Abundant under rocks. Puget Sound to southern California. LTZ, IR.

Class Gastropoda—Snails, limpets, nudibranches, etc.
Subclass Prosobranchia
Order Archaeogastropoda—Limpets, abalones, turbans

179. Rough Keyhole Limpet, *Diodora aspera.* -59- Shell up to 7 cm (2¾") long with a small round or oval hole at the top; many radiating ribs, every fourth rib larger. Color gray, with grayish-brown rays. Often with the commensal scale worm, *Arctonoe vittata,* found under the shell. Surf-washed rocks. Alaska to Baja. LTZ, OR.

180. Volcano-Shell Limpet, *Fissurella volcano.* Shell 2–3.5 cm (¾–1⅛") long. Looks like its name. Prettily marked, pink with black or reddish brown rays; yellow foot. Crescent City to Baja. HTZ, IR in south, but drops to LTZ in north.

181. Giant Keyhole Limpet, *Megathura crenulata.* Body extends out of shell and is up to 25 cm (9¾") long; buff or pink shell up to 13 cm (5"), largely covered by black mantle; foot yellow. Monterey to Baja. LTZ, OR.

182. Black Abalone, *Haliotis cracherodii.* Up to 20 cm (8") long. Shell exterior usually shiny and without any plant growth, dark green, dark blue, or black; interior iridescent green and pink; 5–7 open holes on shell. In crevices and under rock ledges. Mendocino Co., California, to Baja. HTZ to LTZ, OR.

183. Red Abalone, *Haliotis rufescens.* -14- Up to 30 cm (12") long. Shell exterior brick-red, sculptured with low, irregular, radiating ridges; 3–4 open holes; often overgrown by fouling organisms. In rocky areas with heavy surf. Sunset Bay, Oregon, to Baja. LTZ, OR.

184. Green Abalone, *Haliotis fulgens.* Length up to 25 cm (9¾"), usually less than 20 cm (8"). Shell exterior olive green to reddish brown; often overgrown; 5–7 open holes; interior very iridescent, dark green and blue colors. Point Conception to Baja. LTZ, OR.

185. Pink Corrugated Abalone, *Haliotis corrugata.* Length up to 25 cm (9¾"), but usually around 15 cm (6"). Shell arched in adults, usually with scalloped margin, and with irregular diagonal

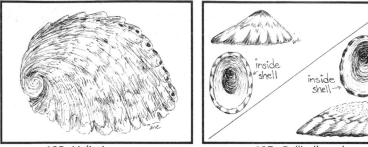

185. *Haliotis corrugata*

187. *Collisella pelta*
188. *Collisella digitalis*

rows of corrugations; exterior greenish or reddish brown, often covered with fouling marine organisms; interior iridescent pink and green; 2–4 open holes. Prefers quiet, more sheltered water. Point Conception, California, to Baja. Common on rocks in beds of offshore *Macrocystis* kelp. Less common LTZ, IR.

186. Japanese Abalone, *Haliotis kamtschatkana.* To about 15 cm (6") long. Pinkish shell with 5 open holes. Flesh yellow-brown. Alaska to Monterey. LTZ, IR.

Superfamily Patellacea—True limpets

187. Shield Limpet, *Collisella pelta.* Up to 4 cm (1½") long. Shell exterior highly variable in color: brown, green, to black are common, often checkered or rayed with white; texture ridged or smooth. Alaska to Baja. MTZ, LTZ, IR and OR.

188. Ribbed Limpet, *Collisella digitalis.* -10- From 1.5–3 cm (½–1¼") long. Dingy brown or olive green with white blotches; apex of shell pointed far forward and may even have an overhang; has noticeable ribs or ridges. One of the most common rock limpets on the Pacific Coast. Favors vertical or overhanging rock faces. Alaska to s. Baja. SPLZ, HTZ, IR.

189. Rough Limpet, *Collisella scabra.* -11- Shell up to 3 cm (1⅛") long; low profile; apex well forward of center; strongly ribbed with scalloped margin; exterior mottled greenish or brown, white to gray where eroded. Common on gently sloping to horizontal rocks. Cape Arago, Oregon, to s. Baja. SPLZ, HTZ, IR.

190. File Limpet, *Collisella limatula.* Shell 3–4.5 cm (1⅛–1¾") long; low profile; filelike, fine radial ribs; margin has sawtooth notching; exterior yellow, buff, or greenish brown, occasionally with darker markings; sides of

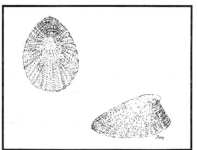

190. *Collisella limatula*

191. Collisella asmi
194. Notoacmea persona

195. Notoacmea depicta
196. Notoacmea paleacea

foot characteristically black or gray. Abundant on semiprotected rocks. Newport, Oregon, to s. Baja. MTZ, LTZ, IR.

191. Black Turban Limpet, *Collisella asmi.* Shell up to 1 cm (³⁄₈") long, and almost as high; dark brown or black. Usually found living commensally on turban snails, Tegula. British Columbia to Mexico. HTZ, MTZ, IR.

192. Coralline Algae or **Triangular Limpet,** *Collisella triangularis.* Up to 7 mm (¹⁄₄") long. Recognized by its habitat, living on coralline. Exterior white, with pinkish to brown spots or rays; often itself covered with coralline algae. Alaska to Baja. LTZ, IR.

193. Seaweed Limpet, *Notoacmea insessa.* Shell up to 2.2 cm (⁷⁄₈") long, higher than wide; outside dark brown, shiny and smooth. Commonly clinging to the flat blades of feather boa kelp, *Egregia menziesii,* on which it feeds. Alaska to Baja. LTZ, IR.

194. Mask Limpet, *Notoacmea persona.* Average size 3.4 cm (1³⁄₈") long. Like *C. digitalis* one side of the shell is very steep, the top seeming to lean forward, but not as far as in the other one. Exterior olive green with white dots sprinkling the surface. Found in deep crevices and dark places. Comes out to feed at night. Alaska to Morro Bay, California. SPLZ, HTZ, IR.

195. Eelgrass or **Painted Limpet,** *Notoacmea depicta.* Up to 1.2 cm (¹⁄₂") long. Narrow shell pale, with radiating brown streaks. Common on blades of eelgrass, *Zostera,* in quiet bays. Los Angeles Co., California, to s. Baja. LTZ, IR.

196. Surfgrass or **Chaffy Limpet,** *Notoacmea paleacea.* Up to 1 cm (³⁄₈") long. Narrow body clings to surfgrass, *Phyllospadix,* on which it is commonly found. Exterior light brown, top white where the covering has been worn away. Vancouver Island to Baja. LTZ, IR.

197. Plate Limpet, *Notoacmea scutum.* Up to 6.3 cm (2¹⁄₂") long. The flattest of the limpets. Often brownish or greenish with white spots or lines, sometimes with stringers of green algae, *Ulva* and *Enteromorpha.* An active limpet that will vigorously flee contact with a predator seastar. Alaska to Point Conception, California. MTZ, IR.

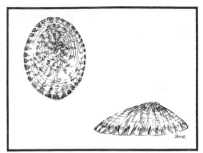

197. *Notoacmea scutum*

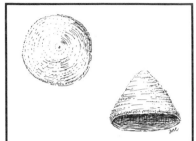

198. *Acmaea mitra*

200. *Astraea gibberosa*

201. *Astraea undosa*

202. *Calliostoma annulatum*

205. *Tegula brunnea*

198. White-Cap or **Dunce-Cap Limpet**, *Acmaea mitra*. Up to 3.5 cm (1⅜") long and nearly as high. White, conical, with apex almost at center. Often encrusted with red coralline algae. Its empty shells are frequently tossed up on beaches by the waves. Alaska to Baja. LTZ, IR.

199. Owl Limpet, *Lottia gigantea*. -60- Up to 9 cm (3½") long, usually less. Very large, brown limpet, with white marks. Leaves a large scar on rock. Interior bluish muscle scar has a prominent owl-shaped marking. Common on cliff faces and rocks of surf-swept coasts. Neah Bay, Washington, to Baja. SPLZ to MTZ, OR.

Superfamily Trochacea—Turban and top snails

200. Red Top Snail, *Astraea gibberosa*. Up to 7.5 cm (3") diameter in British Columbia, to 5 cm (2") in California. Red, cone-shaped shell covered with brownish periostracum (protective outer cover); distinctive whorls with a regular pattern of bumps lie between intersecting spiral and diagonal grooves. Large top shells are often overgrown with algae or hydroids, making them hard to see. On rocks. British Columbia to Baja. LTZ, IR.

201. Wavy Top Snail, *Astraea undosa*. Up to 11 cm (4¼") diameter. Heavy cone-shaped, tan shell has large regular whorls distinguished by wavy vertical ridges. More common subtidally in kelp beds. Point Conception to central Baja. LTZ, IR.

202. Purple-Ringed Top Snail, *Calliostoma annulatum*. Up to 3 cm (1⅛") diameter. Surface nearly evenly conical with beaded spiral ridges. Yellow to orange-brown with a purple band along the beaded spiral; foot bright orange or yellow. Common on giant offshore kelps. Alaska to Baja. LTZ, IR, OR.

203. Channeled Top Snail, *Calliostoma canaliculatum*. Diameter up to 3.5 cm(1⅜"). Shell sharply conical, pale brown or white with darker spiral ridges; foot tan. Common on offshore giant kelps. Alaska to Baja. LTZ, IR, OR.

204. Blue Top Snail, *Calliostoma ligatum*. -12- Width up to 2.5 cm (1"). Conical, chestnut brown with light tan spiral ridges. Blue inner pearly layer sometimes shows through to the outside; foot orange with dark brown sides. Alaska to Baja. LTZ, IR, OR, but more frequently on offshore kelp.

205. Brown Turban Snail, *Tegula brunnea*. Up to 3 cm (1⅛") diameter; roundly conical, smooth. Shell orange or bright brown; foot whitish with dark brown or black sides. Cape Arago, Oregon, to s. California. MTZ, LTZ, IR.

206. Black Turban Snail, *Tegula funebralis*. -13- Up to 3 cm (1⅛") diameter. Shell dark purple to black, white below. Turban shells often become dingy gray when dry. Sometimes shows pronounced spiral ridges. Vancouver Island to central Baja. HTZ, MTZ, IR.

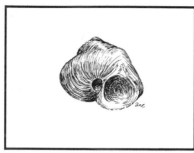

208. *Norrisia norrisi*

209. *Crepidula adunca*

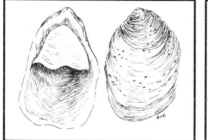

211. *Crepidula nummaria*

212. *Serpulorbis squamigerus*

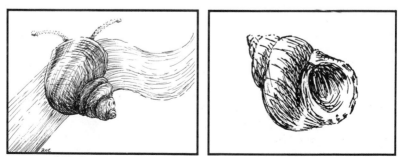

213. *Lacuna porrecta*

214. *Littorina keenae*

207. Beaded Turban Snail, *Tegula eiseni.* About 2.5 cm (1")
wide. Shell brownish colored with raised beaded bands. Common
in rubble and on rocks. Hides from daylight. Los Angeles Co., California, to Baja. MTZ, LTZ, IR.

208. Smooth Turban Snail, *Norrisia norrisi.* Up to 5 cm (2")
diameter. Bright red flesh of foot contrasts with lustrous brown of
shell; sometimes black at base. Frequently a pink slipper snail,
Crepidula norrisiarum, will be found attached to the larger animal's
shell. Point Conception to Baja. LTZ, IR.

Order Mesogastropoda—Cowries, slipper and
moon snails, periwinkles, wentletraps, horn snails, etc.

209. Hooked Slipper Snail, *Crepidula adunca.* Shell up to 2.5
cm (1") long. Small dark brown, oval-shaped shell with a sharply
recurved, hooklike apex. Usually found clinging to a turban shell,
especially *Tegula funebralis.* British Columbia to Baja. MTZ, IR.

210. Pink Slipper Snail, *Crepidula norrisiarum.* Tiny limpet that
rides on *Norrisia norrisi* (208 above). It is occasionally found on
other shells or even on a crab. LTZ, IR.

211. White Slipper Snail, *Crepidula nummaria.* To over 4 cm
(1½") long. Has much variation in shape and size due to clinging to
larger shells of different kinds. Shell white with a thick, rough, yellowish brown periostracum; apex overhangs margin. In holes, under
rocks, and in unoccupied shells. Alaska to s. California. LTZ, IR.

212. Fixed Tube Snail, *Serpulorbis squamigerus.* Lives in tubes
that look exactly like worm tubes, but can be recognized because
the head retracts into the tube slowly, unlike worm heads, which
snap back quickly. Tube diameter to 1.2 cm (½") and up to 12.5
cm (5") long, twisted and wrinkled with longitudinal ribs, gray to
pinkish gray. Feeds by secreting a mucus in which it traps small
organisms. Numerous tubes of these snails mesh together on rocks.
Monterey Bay to Baja. MTZ, IR.

213. Wide-Chink Snail, *Lacuna porrecta.* About 5 mm (³⁄₁₆")
tall. Noted for comparatively large aperture and large umbilical
chink. Has ducklike waddle when it moves. Alaska to San Diego.
Common on eelgrass of bays and estuaries.

214. Eroded Periwinkle, *Littorina keenae* (formerly *L. planaxis*).
Up to 2 cm (¾") high, usually less. Surface often eroded and faintly
lined; broad and conical with 3 whorls. Dingy gray color, sometimes
with white spots. Interior of aperture brown with a white band curving
inward at base; inner lip flattened. Some species of *Littorina* can survive outside a marine environment for long periods of time. Cape
Arago, Oregon, to Baja. Abundant on rocks in SPLZ; HTZ also, IR.

215. Checkered Periwinkle, *Littorina scutulata.* Shell up to 13
mm (½") high. Daintier and slimmer than *L. keenae* and has one
more whorl; shell often checkered white on shining black or

brown. Aperture purplish within. Alaska to Baja. Very common in HTZ and upper MTZ, IR.

216. Sitka Periwinkle, *Littorina sitkana.* Slightly smaller than *L. keenae,* and replacing it as the common periwinkle on high tide zone rocks north of Cape Arago, Oregon. Strong shell with 5 spiral ridges and whorls; nearly circular, gaping aperture. Prefers damp, sheltered crevices. Alaska to Cape Arago, Oregon. SPLZ, HTZ, IR.

216. Littorina sitkana	*217. Trichotropis cancellata*

217. Checkered Hairy Snail, *Trichotropis cancellata.* Shell up to 2.4 cm (1") long. Longitudinal ribs cross the spiral ones. Hairy covering of shell is a light brown or gray; aperture often pink. Alaska to Oregon. LTZ, IR. Also rocky shores of bays and estuaries.

218. Sculptured Wentletrap, *Opalia funiculata.* Shell up to 2 cm (³⁄₄") tall, with 14 broad, weak axial ribs; white to golden yellow. Common around the bases of sea anemones. Santa Barbara, California, to Peru. LTZ, IR.

Order Neogastropoda—Cones, rock snails, whelks, olives, etc.

219. Variegated Amphissa, *Amphissa versicolor.* Shell up to about 1.7 cm (⅝"); axial ribs slantwise to whorls, crossed by close-set spiral cords. Color variable: white, yellow, brown, etc., often mottled. Unlike most snails *Amphissa* is very active and quick, and often imitates an attacking hermit crab. Undersides of rocks in gravel. Fort Bragg, California, to Baja. MTZ, LTZ, IR.

218. Opalia funiculata	*219. Amphissa versicolor*

220. *Ceratostoma foliatum*   221. *Conus californicus*

220. Leafy Hornmouth, *Ceratostoma foliatum*. Shell up to 10 cm (4") high, usually less than 8 cm (3"). Distinguished by three projecting, flowerlike flanges on the largest whorl and a tooth on the outer lip of the aperture; exterior gray or white to yellow-brown. On rock surfaces. Actively carnivorous. From Alaska to San Diego, but rare south of Point Conception. LTZ, IR.

221. California Cone Snail, *Conus californicus*. Up to 4 cm (1½") high, conical, with short spire and narrow aperture. Shell grayish brown with reddish brown periostracum. Snail's radula, or long, prehensile tongue, has a poison tooth on the end used to catch and paralyze prey. (Not harmful to humans.) On rocky and sandy bottoms. San Francisco to Baja. LTZ, IR.

222. Oregon Hairy Triton, *Fusitriton oregonensis*. Up to 15 cm (6") high. Our largest intertidal rock snail. Shell light brown, covered with gray-brown, bristly periostracum; 6 whorls. Preys aggressively on other mollusks and sea urchins. Alaska to s. California. LTZ, IR.

223. Japanese Oyster Drill, *Ceratostoma inornatum*. Shell has very horny, ridged whorls. Snail is an active predator of Pacific oysters. Originally from Japan, it is now naturalized in Tomales Bay, California, and Puget Sound. LTZ, IR.

224. Emarginate Dogwinkle, *Nucella emarginata*. Up to 4 cm (1½") high, usually 3 cm (1") or less; low spire; color variable, often with alternating light and dark spiral bands; spiral

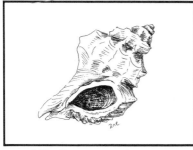 

223. *Ceratostoma inornatum*   224. *Nucella emarginata*

225. *Acanthina spirata*   226. *Haminoea vesicula*

ridges vary from nearly smooth to pronounced. In ancient times this snail was reputedly used to make purple dye. On rocky shores with strong to slight surf. Alaska to n. Baja. HTZ, MTZ, OR.

225. Angular Unicorn, *Acanthina spirata.* Shell up to 4 cm (1½") high, pale blue-gray, with prominent keel at the shoulders; spiral rows of black spots. Found on protected rocks and pilings. Tomales Bay (Marin Co., California) to Baja. HTZ, MTZ, IR

Subclass Opisthobranchia
Order Cephalaspidea

226. White Bubble Snail, *Haminoea vesicula.* Shell oval, up to 2 cm (¾") long, usually half that; fragile; translucent, whitish or greenish yellow; too small to contain the comparatively large body. Burrows just below the surface of mud or sand. Seasonally abundant on mud flats and sandy mud areas of bays. Alaska to Gulf of California.

Order Anaspidea

227. California Sea Hare, *Aplysia californica.* Usually 13–26 cm (5–10") long, but may reach 40 cm (16"). Mature animals reddish, brownish and/or greenish, often with darker splotches, and network of dark lines; 4 tentacles on head; shell is inside the body. A herbivore which feeds mainly on various algae and on eelgrass. Found from mud flats to semi-exposed wavestruck shores. N. California to Gulf of California. MTZ, LTZ, IR.

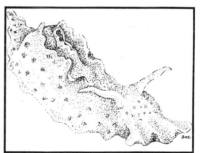

227. *Aplysia californica*

228. Taylor's Sea Hare, *Phyllaplysia taylori.* From 2.5–4.5 cm (1–1¾") long; bright green with brown-black and white stripes and spots. Resembles a nudibranch. Lives exclusively on blades of eelgrass. British Columbia to San Diego. LTZ in bays and estuaries.

Order Notaspidea

229. Yellow Sponge Tylodina, *Tylodina fungina*. This small yellow creature (about 3.5 cm/1⅜" long) looks like a soft-shelled limpet, with its limpetlike "thatched" shell, but is related to the sea hare. Has two front antennae; crawls primarily on yellow sponges. San Luis Obispo Co. to Mexico. LTZ, IR.

Order Nudibranchia—Nudibranches

230. Sea Lemon, *Anisodoris nobilis*. Average size around 10 cm (4") but may reach 26 cm (10") long. Brilliant yellow to light orange, with dark background markings between the dorsal tubercles but not on them; 6 branchial gills are white tipped; fruitlike odor. Like most nudibranches, it feeds on various sponges. Alaska to Baja. LTZ, IR.

231. Monterey Dorid, *Archidoris montereyensis*. -61- Usually 2.5–5 cm (1–2") long. Bright yellow to yellow-orange with dark spots scattered along the back, some on the tubercles, unlike *Anisodoris*; 7 branchial gills. Alaska to San Diego. LTZ, IR.

232. Yellow-Edged Cadlina, *Cadlina luteomarginata*. Usually 2.5–4 cm (1–1½") long, sometimes up to 8 cm (3⅛"). Whitish to light yellow with lemon yellow tubercule tips and body margins. Vancouver Island to Baja. LTZ, IR.

233. Hopkin's Rose, *Hopkinsia rosacea*. -62- Average size 3 cm (1⅛") long. Brilliant rose-pink with numerous long, pointed tubercules on back; firm

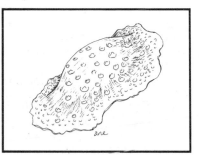

232. *Cadlina luteomarginata*

but fragile, flat body. Feeds primarily on the pink bryozoan, *Eurystomella*. Coos Bay, Oregon, to Baja. LTZ, IR.

234. Blue-and-Gold Nudibranch, *Hypselodoris californiensis*. Up to 6.5 cm (2½") long. Deep blue with many golden yellow spots. Monterey Bay to Gulf of California. LTZ, IR.

235. MacFarland's Chromodoris or **Violet Nudibranch,** *Chromodoris macfarlandi*. Usually less than 3.5 cm (1⅜") long, but may reach 6 cm (2¼"). Distinctive violet, with yellow margin and 3 longitudinal golden yellow stripes. Monterey Bay to Baja. LTZ, IR.

236. Porter's Nudibranch, *Chromodoris porterae*. Usually 1.5–3 cm (½–1⅛") long, smooth, ultramarine colored, with two longitudinal golden yellow stripes. Monterey Bay to Baja. LTZ, IR.

237. Salt-and-Pepper Nudibranch, *Aegires albopunctatus*. From 1–2 cm (⅜–¾") long. Body white to yellowish with opaque salt-and-pepper spots; three small gills. Feeds on white sponges, which closely match its color. Vancouver Island to Baja. LTZ, IR.

238. Shag-Rug Nudibranch, *Aeolidia papillosa*. Often 4–6 cm (1½–2¼") long, sometimes up to 10 cm (4"). Looks like a shag rug with its uniform series of long cerata along each side; feeds mainly on sea anemones and takes on the color of its prey. Alaska to Baja. LTZ, IR.

239. Hooded Nudibranch, *Melibe leonina*. To over 10 cm (4") long. Distinguished by its large elliptical hood, sometimes half the body length; yellowish brown to olive green. Has five or six pairs of flattened, leaflike cerata on its back. When attached to a substratum by its narrow foot, it sweeps the water right and left in search of prey, which it traps with its expanded hood. Alaska to Gulf of California. Common in kelp beds (especially in California) and in eelgrass flats (Puget Sound area).

240. Frost Spot Nudibranch, *Corambe pacifica*. Up to 1 cm (⅜") long, nearly same width; translucent pale body; deep notch in the rear margin; yellowish liver shows through transparent back. Lives and feeds on bryozoan *Membranipora* colonies. Vancouver Island to Baja. LTZ, IR.

241. Ring-Spotted Dorid, *Diaulula sandiegensis*. -63- Body usually under 10 cm (4") but occasionally longer. White or gray to light brown, dotted with a few or many dark rings and spots. Feeds mainly on sponges. Found on large rocks and in tidepools. Alaska to Baja. MTZ, LTZ, IR.

242. Chalk-Lined Dirona, *Dirona albolineata*. Typically 2–4 cm (¾–1½") long, but up to 12 cm (4¾"). Uniformly grayish white, occasionally yellowish to orange. Distinguished by the vivid white lines that trace the margins of its large, arrowhead-shaped cerata. Vancouver Island to San Diego. LTZ, IR.

243. Spotted Dirona, *Dirona picta*. Usually 2–4 cm

242. *Dirona albolineata*

(¾–1½") long, but sometimes up to 10 cm (4"). Color variable: translucent light yellow-green to yellowish brown, dotted with many green, yellow, cream, pink, or brown spots. Large, inflatable cerata each have a pale red spot on the lower outer surface. Cape Arago, Oregon, to Mexico. LTZ, IR.

244. Sea-Clown Nudibranch, *Triopha catalinae*. -64- Body robust, usually 2.5 cm (1") long, but up to 15 cm (6"). Translucent white to pale yellow with bright orange spots; nipplelike appendages also bright orange. Like several other nudibranches, it can move upside down on the surface film of water. Alaska to Baja. MTZ, LTZ, IR.

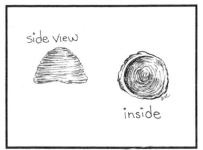

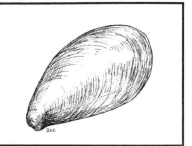

246. *Trimusculus reticulatus*   247. *Mytilus edulis*

245. Spotted Triopha, *Triopha maculata*. Commonly 2–4 cm (³⁄₄–1¹⁄₂″) long; brown, yellowish-brown, or red body sprinkled uniformly with light blue spots; gills and cerata red-orange to red. Humboldt Co., California, to Baja. LTZ, IR.

Subclass Pulmonata

246. Reticulate Button Snail, *Trimusculus reticulatus*. Shell 1–2 cm (³⁄₈–³⁄₄″) diameter, white, sometimes tinged orange, pink, or green; circular and low-arched. Common under overhanging ledges, on the roofs of sea caves, and in crevices and abandoned burrows. Coos Bay, Oregon, to Mexico. MTZ, LTZ, IR.

Class Bivalvia—Clams, mussels, oysters, cockles, etc.
Subclass Pteriomorpha

247. Bay Mussel, *Mytilus edulis*. Shell up to 10 cm (4″) long, usually half that, thin, and bluish black in color. Has finer holding threads than *M. californianus*, so is washed away easier by heavy waves. Wedge-shaped and smooth, lacking radiating ridges. Alaska to Baja. More common in northern half of range. On rocks and wharf pilings. MTZ, LTZ, IR.

248. California Mussel, *Mytilus californianus*. -25- Generally up to 13 cm (5″) long, to 24 cm (9³⁄₈″) along Baja shores. Blue-black, thick, with strong radial ribs and irregular growth lines. Abundant in large beds on surf-exposed rocks. Alaska to southern Baja. HTZ, MTZ. OR mainly, some IR.

249. **Date Mussel,** *Lithophaga plumula.* Shell up to about 5.5 cm (2¹⁄₈″) long. Looks like a brown date because of the glossy brown periostracum, which protects the shell against the strong chemical the mussel secretes to bore into solid rocks for protection. Has two radial grooves extending back from the beaks, with feathery or ridged encrustation on the shell. Mendocino Co., California, to Mexico. LTZ, IR.

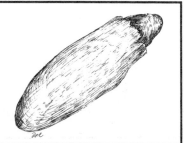

249. *Lithophaga plumula*

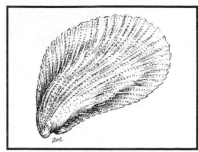

250. *Septifer bifurcatus*

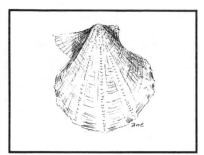

255. *Chlamys hericius*

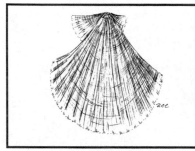

256. *Chlamys hindsii*

257. *Leptopecten latiauratus*

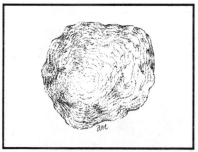

258. *Pododesmus cepio*

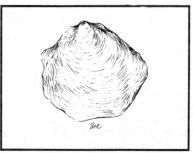

259. *Anomia peruviana*

250. Branch-Ribbed Mussel, *Septifer bifurcatus.* Up to 4.5 cm (1¾") long. Shell wedge-shaped, black, with end beaks pointed. Ridges radiate over surface, becoming wider at posterior end; interior purple. Common under rocks and in crevices. Crescent City, California, to Baja. MTZ, LTZ, IR and OR.

251. Giant Horse Mussel, *Modiolus modiolus.* Up to 23 cm (9") long. Brown to black shell smooth except for coarse beard on the margin. Animal orange or reddish. Alaska to San Pedro. Rare. LTZ, OR.

252. Zig-Zag Horse Mussel, *Musculus senhousia.* Greenish and thin-shelled with zig-zag patterns. Forms large mats on mud flats. Immigrant from Japan. Puget Sound to central California. HTZ, MTZ, IR.

253. Ribbed Horse Mussel, *Ischadium demissum.* Shell up to 10 cm (4") long, brown to black with pronounced radial ribs, scalloped around the lower margin. Interior iridescent and purplish. Forms clusters on rocks and marsh plants in mud flats. San Francisco Bay to Los Angeles harbor. HTZ, MTZ, IR.

254. Giant Rock Scallop, *Hinnites giganteus.* -65- Young shells up to 4.5 cm (1¾") diameter, ribbed, yellowish or orange. Adult shells reach up to 15 cm (6") intertidally; exterior brownish, interior pearly white with a noticeable purple blotch on the center of hinge. Like other scallops, when young, it swims freely by flapping its shells, but in middle age it attaches itself firmly to rocks, shaping itself to their contour, and may become overgrown with algae. Common under rocks and in crevices on the exposed outer coast. British Columbia to Baja. LTZ, OR and IR.

255. Pink Rough-Margined Scallop, *Chlamys hericius.* About 6.3 cm (2½") average diameter. Has prominent rough or spiny radiating ribs; margins rough; upper valve darker pink than lower one. Alaska to San Diego. LTZ, IR.

256. Pink Smooth-Margined Scallop, *Chlamys hindsii.* Smaller in size and with more closely set ribs than *C. hericius.* Ribs of upper valve smooth and nearly equal; margins nearly smooth. Alaska to San Diego. LTZ, IR.

257. Broad-Eared Pecten, *Leptopecten latiauratus.* Shell thin, up to 2 cm (¾") diameter, slightly convex, with wide ears on the hinge. Bright yellow to brown with lighter or darker V-shaped markings. Attached to rocks, pilings, eelgrass in bays. Point Reyes, California, to Baja. LTZ, IR.

258. Abalone Jingle, *Pododesmus cepio.* Shell up to 8 cm (3⅛") diameter, rounded shape, translucent, with irregularly branched, radial ribs. Lower valve thin and contours to substratum; inner surface of upper valve pearly iridescent green. In protected nooks of open shores, on pilings, on red abalone shells. British Columbia to Baja. LTZ, IR and OR.

259. Southern Jingle, *Anomia peruviana.* Similar but smaller than *P. cepio* above. Valves thin and glossy, variable in shape and

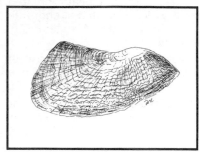

261. *Barnea subtruncata*

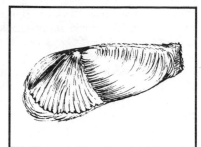

262. *Penitella penita*

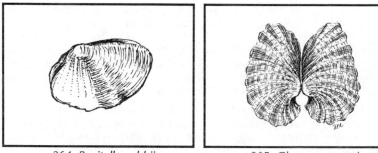

264. *Penitella gabbii*

265. *Glans carpenteri*

266. *Chama arcana*

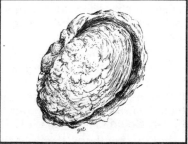

267. *Pseudochama exogyra*

color. All jingles have a hole or notch on the lower valve through which the animal attaches to a rock. They are called "jingles" because of the sound their dead shells make. Central California to Peru. LTZ in quiet bay waters.

260. Native Oyster, *Ostrea lurida.* Shell up to 6 cm (2¼") long; pale gray to bluish black, generally oval, edges sometimes serrated; interior white or greenish yellow; surface rough and scaly. On rocks and pilings in quiet bays and estuaries. Alaska to Baja. LTZ.

Subclass Heterodonta

261. Mud Piddock, *Barnea subtruncata.* Up to 7 cm (2¾") long. Pointed cylindrical shell bores into compact mud or shale. Shell white, marked with distinct and faint radiating ridges. Thin brown periostracum; siphons mottled dark red-brown shading to white at tip. Newport, Oregon, to Chile. LTZ, IR.

262. Flap-Tipped or **Common Piddock,** *Penitella penita.* Up to 7 cm (2¾") long. Globelike front tapers back gradually to where the white shell is covered with a brown periostracum, which continues as a leathery flap past the end of each valve; siphons white and smooth; one plate over the hinge is triangular. Bores into stiff clay, sandstone, and even concrete. Alaska to Baja. MTZ, LTZ, IR and OR.

263. Abalone Piddock, *Penitella conradi.* Shell up to 3.3 cm (1¼") long in rock, 1 cm (⅜") in abalone shells; white, with dark brown periostracum; oval shaped; siphons white. Bores into abalone (especially the red abalone) and mussel shells. Vancouver Island to Baja. LTZ, OR.

264. Small Clay-Boring Piddock, *Penitella gabbii.* Shell up to 5.5 cm (2⅛") long, globular. Siphons up to twice length of shell, white to creamy lemon colored, and covered with distinct tubercles. Bores into stiff clay or shale. Alaska to San Pedro, California. LTZ, IR and OR.

265. Little Heart Clam, *Glans carpenteri.* 1.5 cm (⅝") long. Cocklelike, rectangular shell with 14 to 17 strong, beaded, radiating ribs. Color tan to whitish with brown, pink or yellowish markings. Undersides of rocks. British Columbia to Baja. LTZ, IR.

266. Agate Chama or **Fixed Clam,** *Chama arcana.* Up to 6 cm (2¼") diameter, often taller than long. Heavy, strong white shell, sometimes tinged with red, pink, or orange; both valves are covered with rough concentric frills, reminiscent of agate; upper valve smaller and nearly flat. Undersurfaces of protected rocks and pilings. Oregon to Baja. MTZ, LTZ, IR.

267. Reversed Chama, *Pseudochama exogyra.* Up to 5 cm (2") diameter. Always attached by right (lower) valve to rock, which is the reverse of *Chama arcana*; also with fewer frills. Color dull white, sometimes greenish. Beaks coil to the left instead of right as in *C. arcana*, when viewed from above. Oregon to s. Baja. MTZ, LTZ, IR.

268. Checked Borer, *Platyodon cancellatus.* Shell up to 7 cm (2¾") long, whitish. Fine concentric lines on the anterior end, truncated and wide open at the posterior end; periostracum thick at the margins; siphons long and darkly pigmented with two pointed plates near the tip. Bores into banks of hard blue clay or soft sandstone. British Columbia to San Diego. MTZ, IR.

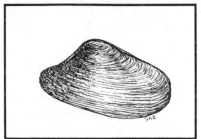 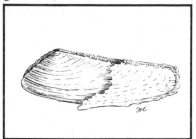

268. Platyodon cancellatus   *269. Hiatella arctica*

269. Little Gaper Clam, *Hiatella arctica.* Shell up to 5 cm (2") long, chalky white; periostracum yellowish with a row of prickles; siphons redtipped. Often distorted in shape to fit surroundings. Can bore into soft rock or nestles in rock crevices. Alaska to Panama. LTZ, IR

270. Common Littleneck Clam, *Protothaca staminea.* Shell up to 7 cm (2¾") long, whitish or tan with angular pattern of brown, distinct radiating ribs crossed by many weak, concentric lines. Abundant burrowing shallowly in coarse or muddy sand in bays and estuaries, and in gravel under rocks along open shores. Alaska to Baja. MTZ, LTZ, IR.

271. Japanese Littleneck Clam, *Tapes japonica.* Shell up to 5 cm (2") long. Similar to the common littleneck but smaller. Color variable but often yellow or buff with lines of brown or black; radiating ribs are crossed by weaker concentric ridges. Found in sandy mud of bays and estuaries. Introduced from Japan. British Columbia to s. California. MTZ, LTZ, IR.

272. Polished Triangular Clam, *Psephidia lordi.* About 4 mm (⅛") diameter. Polished white or light olive shell, rather triangular in shape. More numerous from Puget Sound north. Rocky shores of bays and estuaries. Alaska to Baja. MTZ, LTZ, IR.

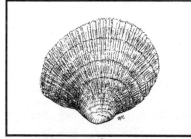 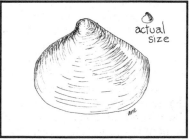

270. Protothaca staminea   *272. Psephidia lordi*

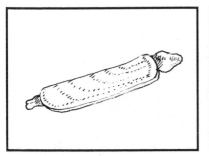

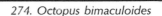

273. Solen sicarius   *274. Octopus bimaculoides*

273. Fast Jackknife Clam, *Solen sicarius*. Shell up to 12.5 cm (nearly 5") long, white, elongate and cylindrical; periostracum glossy greenish yellow or brownish. Rapid digger in mud or eelgrass flats, disappearing in about 30 seconds. Swims forward by forcefully expelling water out of siphons or darts quickly backward by shooting water out of the mantle cavity. It can even jump a few centimeters! Burrows in firm sediments of bays and estuaries, especially in beds of eelgrass. Vancouver Island to Baja. LTZ.

Class Cephalopoda—Octopuses, squids

274. Two-Spotted Octopus, *Octopus bimaculoides*. Dorsal mantle 5–20 cm (2–8") long when mature. Two blue-black, eyelike spots, set farther apart than the real eyes, identify this species. Body color variable: usually brown, gray, reddish, or olive, mottled with black. A sharp black beak is used for defense and offense; shoots out a black ink to disguise itself. In holes and crevices in tidepools. Santa Barbara, California, to Mexico. MTZ, LTZ, IR.

275. Giant Pacific Octopus, *Octopus dofleini*. Smaller animals of this species are occasionally found in the low intertidal zone. Body ovoid, with extensive skin folds, red to reddish brown above, pale below, and without the two dark eye-spots of *O. bimaculoides*. The largest specimen recorded had a total arm span of 9.6 meters (almost 32') and weighed 272 kilograms! Alaska to California. LTZ, IR.

Phylum Echinodermata—Seastars, brittle stars, sea urchins, sea cucumbers

Class Asteroidea—Seastars

276. Bat Star or **Sea Bat**, *Patiria miniata*. -1 - Arm radius up to 10 cm (4"). Its common name comes from its short webbed rays, usually 5 (sometimes 4–9). Color variable: purple to red to yellow, mottled or plain. Common on or under rocks overgrown with surfgrass, algae, etc. Alaska to Baja. MTZ, LTZ, IR.

277. Ochre or **Common Seastar**, *Pisaster ochraceus*. -25- Arm radius up to 28 cm (11"), but normally half this size. Body purple, brown, orange, or yellow with small white spines forming a netlike

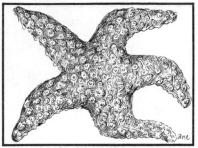 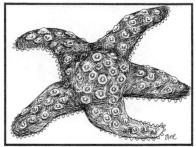

278. *Pisaster giganteus*   279. *Pisaster giganteus capitatus*

pattern. Usually 5 stout, tapering rays, sometimes 4–7. A strong predator on shellfish. This is the commonest Pacific Coast Seastar. On rocks. Alaska to Baja. HTZ to LTZ, OR.

278. Giant Seastar, *Pisaster giganteus.* Arm radius to over 30 cm (12") subtidally. Spines fewer and larger than on *P. ochraceus.* Body red, purple, brown, or tan, with blue rings around the base of the spines; arms thick. Intertidal members of this species are not "gigantic" but typically smaller than the common *P. ochraceus.* Vancouver Island to Baja. LTZ, IR.

279. Southern Giant Seastar, *Pisaster giganteus capitatus.* Similar size to *P. giganteus.* Bright, slaty purple spines contrast to a background of ochre. Spines even larger and more stumpy than in *P. giganteus.* San Luis Obispo, California, to Baja. LTZ, IR.

280. Pink Short-Spined Seastar, *Pisaster brevispinus.* -26- Arm radius to 32 cm (12½"). Pink in color and soft bodied; spines much smaller than those on other *Pisaster* species. Usually on sand or mud bottoms, sometimes on rocks or pilings in quiet water. Alaska to Mission Bay, California. LTZ, IR.

281. Delicate Six-Rayed Seastar, *Leptasterias pusilla.* -27- Arm radius up to 2.2 cm (⅞"). Light gray-brown (sometimes reddish), and clean-cut appearance; spines long and thin. Common in tidepools containing seaweed and exposed to sunlight. Central California. MTZ, IR.

282. Six-Rayed Seastar, *Leptasterias hexactis.* Arm radius up to 5.2 cm (2"). Similar to *L. pusila,* but rays are broader, with flattened, mushroom-shaped spines. Upper surface usually brown or black, sometimes red or greenish. British Columbia to s. California. MTZ, LTZ, IR, OR.

283. Red Seastar, *Henricia leviuscula.* -66- Arm radius up to 9 cm (3½"), usually less. Bright red to tan, or purplish, often banded with darker shades; long, tapering rays. On protected sides of rocks, under rocks, and in pools. Alaska to Baja. LTZ, IR.

284. Pacific Comet Star, *Linckia columbiae.* Arm radius up to 9 cm (3½"). Color usually grayish, mottled with red colors. From 1 to 9 rays, normally 5; surface course and granular on both sides. Its common name derives from the amazing capacity of this creature to generate an entirely new seastar from a single autotomized arm, giving it a temporary cometlike appearance. S. California to Mexico. LTZ, IR.

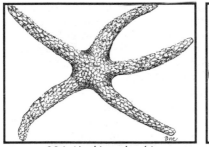

284. *Linckia columbiae*

285. *Astrometis sertulifera*

285. Southern Spiny Seastar, *Astrometis sertulifera*. Arm radius up to 8 cm (3⅛"); flexible; upper surface green to brown and slightly slimy. Long spines blue, purple, or orange with red tips; tube feet yellow or white. Common on sand, rocks, and kelp holdfasts. Santa Barbara to Gulf of California. LTZ, IR.

286. Leather Star, *Dermasterias imbricata*. Arm radius up to 12 cm (4¾"). Smooth, slippery skin feels like wet leather; blue-gray mottled with red or orange. Slightly webbed rays and a large, high disk. Tips of arms frequently upturned; often has a strong garlic odor. Alaska to San Diego. LTZ, IR.

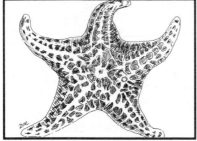

286. *Dermasterias imbricata*

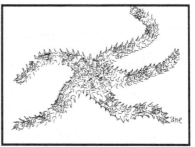

288. *Orthasterias koehleri*

287. Troschel's Seastar, *Evasterias troschelii*. Arm radius up to 20.5 cm (8"). Similar in appearance to the common seastar, *Pisaster ochraceous,* but with more slender arms and a smaller disk. Color orange or brown to blue-gray. Distinguished from *P. ochraceous* by tiny pedicellariae bordering the grooves through which the tube feet are extended. Alaska to Monterey Bay, but rare south of Puget Sound. Likes quieter waters of bays and estuaries, and is more often subtidal. LTZ, IR.

288. Fragile Spiny Seastar, *Orthasterias koehleri*. Arm radius up to 21 cm (8¼"). Fragile; small disk and 5 slender arms. Conspicuous sharp spines light purple to white. Upper surface varies from bright red mottled with yellow to rosy pink mottled with gray.

Prefers quiet waters. Alaska to s. California. Common subtidally, but occasionally LTZ.

289. Sunflower Star, *Pycnopodia helianthoides.* -28- Arm radius up to 40 cm (16") or more. This is the largest and fastest moving of the Pacific Coast seastars. Broad disk is soft and flexible with up to 24 rays, usually purple, pink, or brown in color (sometimes red, orange, or yellow). The supreme carnivore of the lower tidepools, it kills and eats sea urchins, snails, and anything else it can overpower. Alaska to s. California. LTZ, IR.

290. Dawson's Sun Star, *Solaster dawsoni.* Arm radius up to 16 cm (6¼") or more. Usually 12 arms, but varies from 8 to 15. Color gray, cream, yellow, or brown, sometimes red or orange, often with lighter patches. Alaska to Monterey Bay. LTZ, IR.

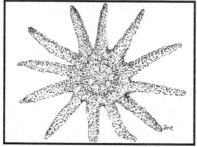

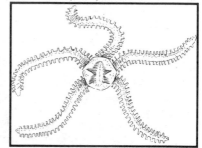

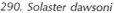
290. *Solaster dawsoni*

292. *Amphipholis pugetana*

291. Stimpson's Sun Star, *Solaster stimpsoni.* Arm radius up to 8.2 cm (3¼"). Commonly with 10 arms, slim and uniformly tapering; upper surface red, orange, yellow, green, or blue. A blue-gray stripe runs up the center of each ray to join as a spot on the central disk. Both these sun stars are harder skinned and have a less webbed appearance than the sunflower star. *S. stimpsoni* is the primary prey of *S. dawsoni.* Alaska to Humboldt Co., California. LTZ, but more frequent in subtidal waters.

Class Ophiuroidea—Brittle stars, or serpent stars

292. Dwarf Brittle Star, *Amphipholis pugetana.* About 2 cm (¾") arm spread in large specimens, ray length 7 to 8 times disk diameter. One of the smallest West Coast brittle stars; gray or banded gray and white. Does not autotomize easily. Very common under rocks. Alaska to Baja. HTZ, MTZ, IR.

293. Snaky-Armed Brittle Star, *Amphiodia occidentalis.* -29- Disk up to 1.3 cm (½") diameter and smooth; arms very long—10 to 15 times disk diameter—and extremely brittle and thin, with 3 blunt spines on each side of each segment; grayish colored. Will autotomize at the slightest provocation. Hidden under rocks in fine sand most of the time, but brittle stars will surface at night. Alaska to San Diego. MTZ, LTZ, IR.

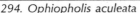
294. *Ophiopholis aculeata*

295. *Ophiothrix spiculata*

294. Daisy Brittle Star, *Ophiopholis aculeata.* Disk diameter up to 2.5 cm (1"), arm length 3 to 4 times that. Color extremely variable (often rusty red) with mottled pattern. Under rocks and in gravel. Alaska to s. California. LTZ, IR.

295. Spiny Brittle Star, *Ophiothrix spiculata.* Disk diameter up to 1.8 cm (⅝"), arm length 5–8 times as long. Tiny spinelets cover disk giving it a fuzzy appearance. Arm spines long, thin, and numerous, set in 7 rows. Color highly variable (often greenish brown with orange bands on the arms). Under rocks and in crevices. San Francisco to Peru. LTZ, IR.

296. Blunt-Spined Brittle Star, *Ophiopteris papillosa.* Disk diameter up to 4.5 cm (1¾"), arm length 3–4.5 times as long. Brown color with darker bands. Spines flat and blunt-tipped. Under rocks and in holdfasts. Vancouver Island to Baja. LTZ, IR.

297. Esmark's Brittle Star, *Ophioplocus esmarki.* Disk diameter up to 3 cm (1⅛"), arms 2–3 times that. Distinguished by solid brown or red-brown color and relatively short, stubby arms with short spines that extend out at an acute angle. Under rocks, in crevices and kelp holdfasts. Tomales Bay, Marin Co., to San Diego. MTZ, LTZ, IR.

298. Panama Brittle Star, *Ophioderma panamense.* Disk up to 4.5 cm (1¾") wide, granular above; arms 3–6 times as long, buff or white banded, with short spines. Color predominantly gray-brown to olive green. San Pedro, California, to Peru. LTZ, IR.

299. Ringed Brittle Star, *Ophionereis annulata.* Disk diameter up to 1.8 cm (⅝"); thin, snakelike arms 7–9 times as long and bear

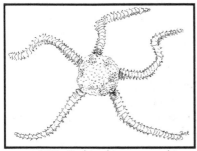

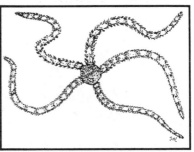

297. *Ophioplocus esmarki*

299. *Ophionereis annulata*

long lateral spines. Color variable (sometimes gray) with dark rings around the arms. Under rocks in sand. San Pedro, California, to Ecuador. LTZ, IR.

Class Echinoidea—Sea urchins, heart urchins, sand dollars

300. Red Sea Urchin, *Strongylocentrotus franciscanus*. -21- Test (shell) diameter often more than 10 cm (4"), bristling spines 5 cm (2") or more in length; brick-red or purple in color. Looks like a circular porcupine. The urchins are armed with pedicellariae (tiny pincerlike structures) containing poison glands used to ward off the attack of predators, like the seastar. Alaska to Baja. LTZ, IR and OR.

301. Purple Sea Urchin, *Strongylocentrotus purpuratus*. -22-

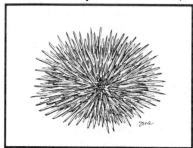

301. Strongylocentrotus purpuratus

Test diameter from 5–10 cm (2–4"). Seeks burrows or depressions on tidepool rocks or under seaweeds; prefers strong wave action. Spines are shorter and blunter than in *S. franciscanus* and vividly purple, occasionally greenish tinged with purple. Both species like to feed on a variety of brown and red algae, especially the kelp, *Macrocystis*. Vancouver Island to Baja. LTZ, OR.

302. Green Sea Urchin, *Strongylocentrotus droebachiensis*. Test up to 8 cm (3") wide. Spines light green, rarely brownish green. Prefers quiet bay waters. Puget Sound north to Alaska LTZ, IR.

303. Gray Sea Urchin, *Lytechinus anamesus*. Test up to 4 cm (1½") wide, thin, and domed. Juvenile specimens are pale; mature individuals cream-colored to dull gray-purple with purplish patches on the upper surface. Often clusters in large groups. Rocky shores and on eelgrass in Baja bays; sandy bottoms in deep pools. Channel Islands to Gulf of California. LTZ, IR.

Class Holothuroidea—Sea cucumbers

304. Tar Spot Sea Cucumber, *Cucumaria pseudocurata*. Up to 3.5 cm (1⅜") long. Resembles a small piece of tar sticking to the rocks.

305. Cucumaria lubrica

Dark brown to black above; has 10 highly branched tentacles. Wide range of habitat: in beds of coralline algae, underneath mats of seaweed, and in mussel beds. British Columbia to Monterey Bay. HTZ to LTZ, IR and OR.

305. Brown-Dotted Sea Cucumber, *Cucumaria lubrica*. From 5–10 cm (2–4") long, cylindrical. Whitish skin has brown dots or blotches, sometimes nearly covering the surface. Alaska to Monterey Bay, but rarer in south of range. Rocky shores. LTZ, IR.

306. Red Sea Cucumber, *Cucumaria miniata.* From 10–25 cm (4–10") in length. Usually brick red, but ranging from pale pink to purple. Has 10 bright orange, highly branched feeding tentacles of equal size. 5 rows of tube feet, 2 above, 3 below. Under rocks and in crevices. Alaska to Monterey Bay, but rare south of Sonoma Co. LTZ, IR.

307. Black-Dotted Sea Cucumber, *Chiridota albatrossi.* From 12–15 cm (4³⁄₄–6") long. Sluglike and slim, covered with peppery black dots; smooth skin except for white calcareous granules. Southwestern Alaska, mainly in quiet bay waters. LTZ, IR.

308. Stiff-Footed Sea Cucumber, *Eupentacta quinquesemita.* -67- From 4–10 cm (1¹⁄₂–4") long, cylindrical, white or cream colored. 5 rows of long, stiff, non-retractable tube feet make the creature look bristly; 10 short, yellow, bushy feeding tentacles. Under rocks and in crevices. Alaska to Baja. LTZ, IR.

309. Common White Synapta, *Leptosynapta albicans.* From 5–15 cm (2–6") long when fully extended; wormlike, with no tube feet. Dirty white to pinkish; 10–12 feathery feeding tentacles. Lacks the respiratory branches of most sea cucumbers, but its semitransparent, delicate skin allows water-dissolved oxygen to enter the body. Skin is smooth but numerous white calcareous granules assist it to move along or burrow in sand or mud under and among rocks. Puget Sound to San Diego. MTZ, LTZ, IR.

310. *Lissothuria nutriens*   311. *Psolus chitonoides*

310. Dwarf Sea Cucumber, *Lissothuria nutriens.* From 1.5–2 cm (¹⁄₂–³⁄₄") long; upper surface bright orange-red; underside pale pink and flattened bearing 3 rows of tube feet; 10 highly branched tentacles. This small sea cucumber is unique for carrying its young on its back. On rocks and in sandy deposits among surfgrass, algae holdfasts, etc. Monterey Bay to s. California. LTZ, IR.

311. Slipper Sea Cucumber, *Psolus chitonoides.* Up to 12 cm (4³⁄₄") long and 6.4 cm (2¹⁄₂") wide; oval and flat-bottomed resembling a slipper. Pale orange to yellow body covered with large, granular plates; crown of 10 highly branched bright red or purple, white-tipped tentacles; rows of tube feet on edges of sole. Alaska to Baja. LTZ, IR.

312. California Sea Cucumber, *Parastichopus californicus*. -68- From 25-40 cm (9¾-15¾") long, cylindrical. This spectacular brown, dark red, or yellow creature can quickly contract or extend its body. Large conical warts cover much of the body, often red-tipped. When disturbed it contracts and may squirt out a strong stream of water. British Columbia to Baja. LTZ, IR.

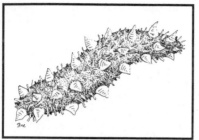

313. Lesser California Sea Cucumber, *Parastichopus parvimensis*. Up to 25 cm (9¾") long, cylindrical. Light chestnut brown above, paler below. Like its relative *P. californicus*, it has conical projections, but smaller and black-tipped. Common on sand and between rocks in quiet waters. Monterey Bay to Baja. LTZ, IR.

312. Parastichopus californicus

314. Shaggy Orange Sea Cucumber, *Pachythyone rubra*. From 2-2.5 cm (¾-1") long. Orange to orange-red above, white below. Body cylindrical, uniformly covered with many tube feet giving it a shaggy appearance; 10 branched tentacles, rarely extended during daylight hours. Likes kelp holdfasts. Monterey Bay to s. California. LTZ, IR.

Phylum Chordata—Animals with a notochord; includes vertebrates

Subphylum Urochordata—Tunicates

Although tunicates externally resemble sponges, they are much higher on the evolutionary scale, possessing a dorsal tubular nerve cord also characterizing vertebrates. They may be distinguished from the latter by their slippery texture. Most sponges have a gritty feeling.

315. California Sea Pork, *Aplidium californicum*. Colonies form sheetlike masses, 15-30 cm (6-12") across and 1-3 cm (⅜-1⅛") thick, with a gelatinous light-colored cover through which the yellowish, orange, or reddish brown zooids can be seen arranged in clusters. Feels soft and mushy; often sandy at base. Common on shaded rocks protected from heavy wave action. Vancouver Island to Baja. MTZ, LTZ, IR.

316. Hard Sheet Tunicate, *Archidistoma psammion*. Colonies form flat sheets up to 20 cm (8") across and 1-2 cm (⅜-

316. Archidistoma psammion

¾") thick, that are stiff but springy, hard and tough, colored purple, maroon, dark brown, or gray; usually covered with some sand. Zooids cluster circularly around evenly distributed shallow craters. On rocks exposed to moderate surf, often with surfgrass. Olympic Peninsula, Washington, to San Diego. LTZ, IR.

317. Brilliant Red Hide Tunicate, *Cnemidocarpa finmarkiensis.* -69- Zooid usually less than 3 cm (1⅛") across the base, hemispherical; outer tunic brilliant red to rose pink, smooth but leathery. Craterlike projections (siphons) bring in water for feeding and respiration. Common on hard surfaces in well-circulated waters. Alaska to Washington, some subtidally to Monterey. LTZ, IR.

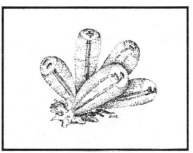

318. *Distaplia occidentalis*   319. *Clavelina huntsmani*

318. Mushroom Tunicate, *Distaplia occidentalis.* Colonies range from 1-10 cm (⅜-4") diameter, frequently mushroom-shaped. Overall colony color highly variable: red, purple, pink, yellow, gray, white, etc. and in combinations of colors. Zooids form rosettes around common craterlike openings. On rocks in well-circulated waters. Vancouver Island to San Diego. LTZ, IR.

319. Light-Bulb Tunicate, *Clavelina huntsmani.* Each zooid is in a separate, transparent light-bulb to club-shaped tube or tunic up to 5 cm (2") long, which often forms dense clusters up to 50 cm (19½") across. Individual clubs connect together at base only. Orange-pink internal organs are visible through the transparent covering. Under ledges and on shaded vertical surfaces. British Columbia to San Diego. LTZ, IR.

320. Slim Club Tunicate, *Euherdmania claviformis.* Tubular zooids up to 6 cm (2¼") long by 2-4 mm (1/16-⅛") thick. Thinner than *C. huntsmani,* also more loosely attached together. Tunic is gray or colorless and often sand-encrusted. Common in beds of surfgrass. Bodega Bay, California, to San Diego. LTZ, IR.

321. Yellow-Green Creeping Tunicate, *Perophora annectens.* Colonies to 10 cm (4")

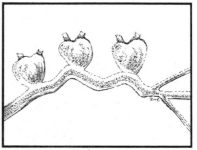

321. *Perophora annectens*

across consist of tiny, yellow-green, globular zooids arising from a network of creeping stems. Easily confused for a plant, but this tunicate's somewhat transparent covering will reveal its working organs inside. On stones, other colonial tunicates, seaweeds, and other substrata in well-circulated waters. San Diego to British Columbia. MTZ, LTZ, IR.

322. Flat-Bulbed Tunicate, *Polyclinum planum*. A large colony consists of a single, flattened, brown bulb up to 20 cm (8") across and 4 cm (1½") thick; usually half this size. The bulb is attached by a thick stalk to the substratum. Clustered zooids give the surface texture a flowery effect. Rocky shores with moderate wave action. Northern California to Baja. LTZ, IR.

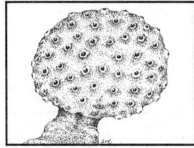
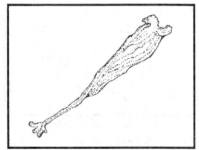

322. *Polyclinum planum*   324. *Styela montereyensis*

323. Decorator Tunicate, *Pyura haustor*. Globular body 5–8 cm (2–3⅛") diameter, usually less; tunic tough and leathery, pale red-tan to ochre-brown. However, color is usually obscure because it decorates itself abundantly with foreign debris. On rocks, pilings, kelp holdfasts, mussel beds, etc. in calm bays to rough open coast. Alaska to San Diego. LTZ, IR and OR.

324. Baseball Club Tunicate, *Styela montereyensis*. Body elongate and cylindrical, resembling somewhat a miniature baseball club, supported by a thinner stalk about equal in length; overall length up to 30 cm (12") in calm bay waters, half that on exposed coast. Tunic yellow to dark red-brown with distinct longitudinal ridges and grooves running the entire length; two siphons: one straight and one recurved. Attaches to solid surfaces, often on wharf pilings. British Columbia to Baja. LTZ, IR and OR.

325. Short-Stalked Baseball Club Tunicate, *Styela gibbsii*. Similar to its relative above, *S. montereyensis*, but smaller and short-stalked. The most common *Styela* of the Puget Sound area. Acts as a host to several sea animals. British Columbia to San Diego. LTZ, IR.

326. Fat Baseball Club Tunicate, *Styela clava*. Body to 15 cm (6") long; similar to *S. montereyensis* but with a fatter body and lacking the former's clear division between body and stalk; tunic usually has conspicuous bumps and irregular longitudinal wrinkles. Color yellow-gray to brownish. In quiet bay waters. San Francisco to San Diego. LTZ, IR.

Subphylum Vertebrata
Class Osteichthyes—
Bony fishes

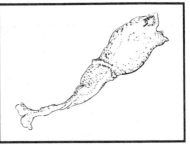

326. Styela clava

327. Black Prickleback, *Xiphister atropurpureus.* Up to 30 cm (12") long; eel-like, no pelvic fins. Young are greenish black, adults almost black, but with traces of dusky whitish or yellowish mottling near tail-end. 2 dark bars with white edges extend down and back from the eyes. Alaska to Baja. Common under rocks. MTZ, LTZ, IR.

328. Rock Prickleback, *Xiphister mucosus.* Up to 58 cm (23") long. Very similar to *X. atropurpureus,* but its 2 dark bars extending down and back from the eyes are bordered by black (not white). Young often pale translucent olive; adults greenish black, gray, or brownish. Alaska to s. California. MTZ, LTZ, IR.

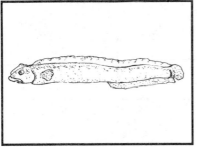

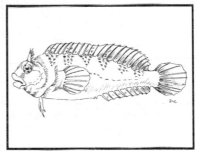

329. Anoplarchus purpurescens   *330. Hypsoblennius gilberti*

329. High Cockscomb, *Anoplarchus purpurescens.* Up to 13 cm (5") long. Distinguished from *Xiphister* above by the fleshy crest on the top of its head and the larger dorsal fin running down the center of its back. Blackish or purple to brown, usually lighter and darker mottling. Under rocks. Alaska to s. California. HTZ to LTZ, IR.

330. Rockpool Blenny, *Hypsoblennius gilberti.* This is a small, unscaled fish up to 17 cm (6¾") long. Skin flap above eye divided into several filaments; dorsal fin long and unnotched with dark saddle markings at its base; body color variable, usually olive to gray. Pt. Conception to s. Baja. MTZ, LTZ, IR.

331. Striped Kelp Fish, *Gibbonsia metzi.* Up to 26 cm (10") long. Reddish to light brown with stripes or darker mottling, matching nearby seaweed. Resembles the rockpool blenny above, but

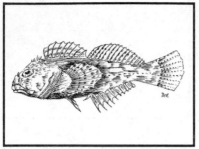

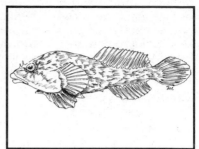

333. *Oligocottus maculosus*

334. *Gobiesox maeandricus*

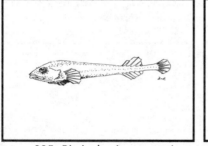

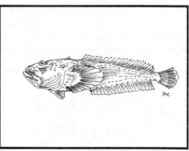

335. *Rimicola eigenamanni*

336. *Porichthys notatus*

337. *Typhlogobius californiensis*

338. *Leuresthes tenuis*

the dorsal fin of kelp fish rises higher at the ends than in the middle. British Columbia to Baja. MTZ, LTZ, IR.

332. Convict Fish or **Painted Greenling**, *Oxylebius pictus*. -38- Length up to 25 cm (10"). 5–7 red or reddish brown bars cross the body and extend onto the fins; background color variable, often grayish to brown; young fish have brilliant blue blotches. Head elongated, almost pointed. Alaska to Baja. LTZ, IR.

333. Tidepool Sculpin or **Rockpool Johnny**, *Oligocottus maculosus*. Small, less than 9 cm (3½") long; skin smooth without scales or prickles. Green to red-brown above, marked with irregular dark saddles on back. Broad, ugly head and tapering body; large pectoral fins. Along rocky shores in tidepools. Alaska to s. California. HTZ to LTZ, IR.

334. Northern Clingfish, *Gobiesox maeandricus*. Up to 16 cm (6½") long. Color variable, gray to brown or red with darker mottling. Wide head tapers quickly to tail giving it a tadpole shape. Slithers over damp, smooth surfaces very rapidly and can cling with considerable strength to rocks using its adhesive sucker disk. Under rocks in tidepools. Alaska to s. California. MTZ, LTZ, IR.

335. Slender Clingfish, *Rimicola eigenamanni*. Up to 5.8 cm (2¼") long; color varies to match surroundings. Slender-bodied, but with broad head and chest. Small suction cup on its breast with which to cling to rocks. San Pedro, California, to s. Baja. MTZ, LTZ, IR.

336. Grunting Fish or **Plainfin Midshipman**, *Porichthys notatus*. Up to 38 cm (15") long. Flattened head with protruding eyes. Makes a grunt when touched or bothered. Has rows of luminescent organs that resemble bright buttons of a naval uniform and can be flashed at will. Rocky shores of estuaries and bays, often hiding under rocks, in crevices, or burrowed in sand. Alaska to s. Baja. LTZ, IR.

337. Blind Goby, *Typhlogobius californiensis*. Up to 8.3 cm (3¼") long. Lives in burrows made by the ghost shrimp; looks like a stubby pink eel. Rudimentary eyes functionless, except when young. Central California to s. Baja. MTZ, LTZ, IR.

338. California Grunion, *Leuresthes tenuis*. Up to 18 cm (7") long. White below, greenish above, with a silvery blue streak in between. At the highest spring tides, it swims up the beach with the breaking waves to the highest point it can reach to deposit its eggs. Under protection of law during April and May, the peak of the spawning period. Sandy beaches. San Francisco to Baja. HTZ, OR.

339. Woolly Sculpin, *Clinocottus analis*. Length up to 18 cm (7"). Grayish green to olive brown above flecked with white, yellow, and pink; dark saddles on back. Clumps and rows of cirri (hairlike projections) on top of head give it a woolly appearance. It usually lies motionless or moves slowly about on the bottom of tidepools. N. California to central Baja. HTZ to LTZ, IR.

340. Opaleye, *Girella nigricans*. Length up to 66 cm (26"). Dark olive gray or green perchlike body usually with two white spots on either side of the dorsal fin; eyes bright blue-green. Swims actively, rarely resting on the bottom. Juveniles enter the tidepools when about 2.5 cm (1") long, but leave for deeper water as they mature. San Francisco to s. Baja. HTZ to LTZ, IR and OR.

341. Hypsypops rubicunda

341. Gold Garibaldi, *Hypsypops rubicunda*. -70- Length up to 36 cm (14"). Distinguished by its solid bright orange to yellow-orange color; eyes green. Juvenile specimens have iridescent blue spots on their red-orange bodies. Lives near rocky bottoms with available crevices and caves. Against the law to collect. Monterey Bay to s. Baja. LTZ, IR.

Suggested References

Flora:

Abbott, Isabella A. and George Hollenberg. *Marine Algae of California*. Stanford: Stanford University Press, 1976.

Guberlet, Muriel Lewin. *Seaweeds at Ebb Tide*. Seattle: University of Washington Press, 1956.

Smith, Gilbert M. *Marine Algae of the Monterey Peninsula*. Stanford: Stanford University Press, 1969.

Fauna:

Eschmeyer, William N., Earl S. Herald, and Howard Hammann. *A Field Guide to Pacific Coast Fishes of North America*. Boston: Houghton Mifflin, 1983.

McLachlan, Dan H. and Jak Ayres. *Fieldbook of Pacific Northwest Sea Creatures*. Happy Camp, California: Naturegraph Publishers, 1979.

Meinkoth, Norman A. *The Audubon Society Field Guide to North American Seashore Creatures*. New York: Alfred A. Knopf, 1981.

Morris, Robert H., Donald P. Abbott, and Eugene C. Haderlie. *Intertidal Invertebrates of California*. Stanford: Stanford University Press, 1980.

Ricketts, Edward F., Jack Calvin, and Joel W. Hedgpeth. *Between Pacific Tides*. rev. David W. Phillips, 5th edition. Stanford: Stanford University Press, 1985.

Index

121

About the Book

First published in 1966 and a popular seller for many years, *Exploring Pacific Coast Tidepools* has now been updated and expanded to include descriptions for 341 different species, of which 184 are portrayed in black and white illustrations and more than 70 in beautiful color photographs. All the scientific and common names have been brought up-to-date and the species information is based on current sources.

This handy field guide to the common seashore fauna and flora of the intertidal zone of the rocky shores covers the Pacific Coast from Alaska to Baja California. Many of the common seashore creatures found in bays and estuaries are also included. Brown's pictorial essay "Adventures and Thrills on Rocky Shores," in which he describes some interesting facts about intertidal life, will succeed in stirring even the most reluctant "couch potato" to go down to the shores to see the colorful and fascinating creatures that live there.

Vinson Brown knows the Pacific Coast tidepools firsthand, having gone on many nature excursions with family and students down to the shore to identify specimens. He was born in Reno, Nevada, and lived most of his life in California. After obtaining his M.A. in biology from Stanford University, Brown distinguished himself as an author, lecturer, and publisher. Of his 40 published books, 29 are in the category of natural history. His lectures to audiences in the United States and Canada have included natural history themes, the preservation of the environment, and Native American cultures.

Illustrator, Ane Rovetta, divides her time between interpreting natural history on field trips and nature walks and drawing wildlife species for nature books and periodicals. Twelve years of her career as a biologist was spent on the Farallon Islands studying elephant seals. Although currently Ane works at Point Reyes National Seashore in California, her work as a freelance naturalist often takes her far afield.